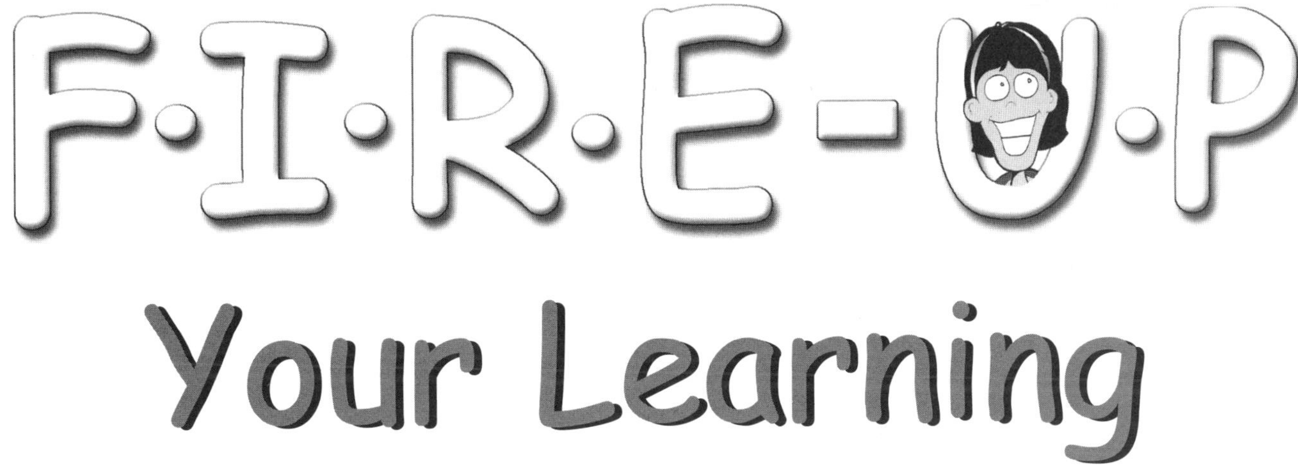

Your Learning

An Accelerated Learning Action Guide

For ages 12 years and up

Thomas L. Madden

First Edition January 2001
Reprint May 2001

Stratigent Press ♦ Las Vegas ♦ Nevada

Published by

Stratigent Press
3900 Paradise Road
Las Vegas, Nevada 89109

Library of Congress Control Numbers; 00-107891

Publisher's - Cataloging-In-Publication

Madden, Thomas, 1949-
Fire-up your learning : an accelerated learning action guide / Thomas L. Madden. -- 1st ed.
p. cm.
LCCN 00-107891
ISBN 0-9702384-0-1

1. Education acceleration--United States--Handbooks, manuals, etc. I. Title.

LB1029.A22M34 2001 153.1'52
QB100-901626

Manufactured in the United States of America
January 2001

Written by: **Thomas L. Madden**
Contributions by: Jayne Nicholl
Artwork by: Patrick J. Stoehr
Layout Design by: Anne Kenyon

Table of Contents

Return On Investment v
Why Make The Investment? v
Rise Above The Crowd vii

INTRODUCTION 1
The Big Picture 3
Daily Record 7
Learning Naturally 9
The Learning Map 13
A Global Look At Each Module 17

MODULE 1 - FOUNDATIONS 21
Building Blocks Of This Module 25
The Methodology 25
Pathways In The Brain 29
    Exercise = Growth 29
The Triune Brain Theory 31
    Three Brains In One 31
Learning And Memory Implications 33
The Mind 37
    The Conscious Mind 39
    The Analytical Mind 41
    The Subconscious Mind 57
    The Instinctive Mind 65
Memory - There Are Five Key Areas Of Memory: 67
    Memory Movement 73
    Memories Can Be Trained 79
    Concentration 81
Study Time Management 85
Studying Text Books 93
Effective Note Taking During Lectures 99

Techniques For Taking Notes 111
Learning Maps 111
Why Do Learning Maps Work So Well? 111
Taking Notes During Interactive Lectures 113
Notes 113
Conclusions 113
Anchors 115
Combining Charts 119

Summary - Module 1 121
It Is Time To FIRE-UP 123

MODULE 2 - INTAKE INFORMATION 125

Overview 129

In And Out Of Style 131

Learning Style Intake 133
Your Sensory Preference 133
Assessing Your Sensory Preferences 134
Results 137

Learning Styles And Sensory Preferences 141

Three Key Learning Styles 143

Visual 145
Learning as a Visual-External Learner 147
Learning as a Visual-Internal Learner 149

Auditory 151
Learning as an Auditory-External Learner 153
Learning as an Auditory-Internal Learner 155

Kinesthetic 157
Learning as a Kinesthetic-External Learner 157
Learning as a Kinesthetic-Internal Learner 161

Multi Sensory Intake 163

Organizational Preferences 165
Global or Linear Organizational Preference 165
Learning as a Global Learner 167
Learning as a Linear Learner 169

Get the "Organized, Big Picture" 171

Hemispheric Preference 173

Summary - Module 2 181

MODULE 3 - REAL MEANING .183
Overview .187
Assimilation Preference .189
Assimilation Preferences Profile .191
Association Assimilators .193
Contrary Assimilators .193
Impetuous Assimilators .195
Scientific Assimilators .195
Social Assimilators .197
Independent Assimilators .197
Summary - Module 3 .199
MODULE 4 - EXPRESS YOUR KNOWLEDGE .201
Overview .205
An Intelligent Person .209
Multiple Task Learning .213
Using Logical Intelligence .213
Number Or Rate Key Concepts .213
Analyze What You Are Learning .213
Using Your Linguistic Intelligence .217
Re-Word Information .217
Using your Interpersonal Intelligence .219
Teach What You've Learned .219
Compare Notes .219
Using your Intra-Personal Intelligence .223
Look For Personal Significance .223
Investigate The Background Information .223
Take Time For Reflection .223
Using Your Musical Intelligence .225
Write A Song, Jingle, Poem or Rap .225
Background Music .227
Using Your Naturalist Intelligence .229
Using Your Spatial Intelligence .231
Creating A Learning Map .231
Create An Image .231
Using your Kinesthetic Intelligence .233
Role-Play .233
The Power Of Writing .235
Sort Your Thoughts .235

Individual Priorities 237
Show You Know Through Practice 239
Testing Yourself 239
Test Yourself With One Of The Following Techniques 241
Catch Yourself Doing Things Right 241
Learning Maps 243
Flashcards 245
Imagination 247
Learning Together 247
Teach Or Tell 249
Role Play 251
Overlapping Information 253
Stepping Stones 255
Summary - Module 4 257
MODULE 5 - USE AVAILABLE RESOURCES 259
Utilize Other People 263
Mentors 265
Teachers or Instructors 265
Learning Partner 265
Family Member or Friend 267
Use Other Resources 267
Use Your New Knowledge 269
Summary - Module 5 271
MODULE 6 - PLAN OF ACTION 277
Elements of Planning - Overview 277
Assessment (Where is the starting point?) 281
The Decision Making Model 283
The Mission Statement (Why?) 285
Goals (What needs to be accomplished?) 291
Responsibilities (Who is required to carry out planned tasks?) 293
Timing (When is the plan to be completed?) 293
Action Items (How are you going to get there?) 293
Flexibility (Re-plan) 295
Summary - Module 6 301
SUMMARY 303
TEST TAKING STRATEGIES 305
Test-Taking Summary 318

F·I·R·E-U·P

Your Learning

Foundations

Intake Information

Real Meaning

Express Your Knowledge

Use Available Resources

Plan of Action

Foundations

Intake Information

Real Meaning

F·I·R·E-U·P

Plan of Action

Express Your Knowledge

Use

Module 1: FOUNDATIONS

- Accelerated Learning
- Your Brain
- Your Mind
- Memory

Module 2: INTAKE INFORMATION

- Learning Style Preferences
- Global/Linear
- Hemisphere Preference

Module 3: REAL MEANING

- Assimilation & Processing Style
- Creating Real Meaning

Module 4: EXPRESS YOUR KNOWLEDGE

- Multiple Intelligences
- Show You Know

Module 5: USE AVAILABLE RESOURCES

- Use New Knowledge
- Utilize Other Resources

Module 6: PLAN OF ACTION

- Reflect, Review & Adjust
- Develop Your Learning Action Plan

+ EFFORT =
LEARNING
WISDOM
KNOWLEDGE

RETURN ON INVESTMENT

Great achievements in life require an input or investment. If a person invests money into the Stock Market, that investor will expect a financial return on that investment.

From the beginning of life until the end, your life grows through learning. You learn to walk, to talk, to think, to evaluate and to make judgments. Your major investment into this program is effort. The more energy and concentration you put into your learning effort, the greater will be the return for a lifetime of learning.

TO DO

AS YOU THINK OF KEY IDEAS, JOT THEM DOWN.

WRITING THEM DOWN WILL REINFORCE THE IDEAS.

WHY MAKE THE INVESTMENT?

These are all questions you should take time to answer NOW.
If you can see more "benefits" from the effort you put into FIRE-UP, you will be motivated to finish the course and gain those benefits.

- **Why are you following this program?**
- **What do you hope to achieve?**
- **What do you see yourself doing after the completion of this program?**
- **What challenges will you face in the learning process?**
- **What action can you take to offset those challenges?**
- **How much time and effort will it take to be successful?**

BENEFITS
WEIGHTS

RISE ABOVE THE CROWD

In the hot air balloon opposite, write as many benefits on the balloon as you can. Think of what you will gain from following your FIRE-UP program. The benefits are represented by the "hot air" that will make your balloon and learning take off.

Just outside the basket beneath the balloon, write all the things that might be classed as "weights". Write the weights in pencil. Weights can at times be "thrown out of the basket" when they are no longer important. Erase weights to throw them away. To ensure your balloon will soar you must have more benefits than weights!

After completing this exercise you will have a graphic representation of your motivation to succeed. If at times during the course of learning, things get a bit tough, you can revisit this picture. Remind yourself of all those benefits you identified as being gained from successfully completing the course.

Remotivated, you will have new energy to carry on and get over the temporary stumbling blocks. You can then continue to FIRE-UP yourself, creating quality, effective learning.

INTRODUCTION

F·I·R·E-U·P Your Learning

Introduction

The Big Picture 3
Daily Record 7
Learning Naturally 9
The Learning Map 13
A Global Look at Each Module 17

Learning is a Skill for Life

THE BIG PICTURE

You will discover your unique learning style and the techniques that will allow you to unlock your extensive brain power.

LEARNING
IS A
SKILL FOR LIFE

Learning in a way that is compatible with the unique way your brain works will extend your capabilities and make learning easier. Effective, flexible, confident learners will be in great demand in the corporate world of tomorrow.

The skill of learning is a skill for life. Subjects advance every day and new learning is needed. With the expertise gained from the FIRE-UP system, you will confidently rise to the challenge of equipping yourself with the skills necessary to stay ahead of the field throughout your life.

Accelerated Learning could be called efficiency learning. Everyone has a great memory. Some people just have deficient recall. The inability to recall information is often caused by "interference" that disrupts the efficient storage of information.

ACCELERATED LEARNING
IS
EFFICIENT LEARNING

Knowing how to FIRE-UP your learning will give you the ability to intake information without interference. Once taken in, the information can be processed, assimilated and output in the most efficient manner.

MISSION

The mission of this program is to give you, the student, tools to maximize your tremendous inborn potential for learning, thinking and creating.

HOW TO USE THIS BOOK

This is your book. You can write in it. You can color. You can doodle. You can draw. It is your book. (Unless this is not your copy! If it is not your book, create your own workbook. Raise your own self-esteem by respecting other people's property.)

As you work your way through the book, there will be times when you must stop and think. Key ideas will arise. You may want to take the time to create a graph or diagram for those ideas.

There will be questions for you to answer. If you do not know the answer to a question, do not be concerned. Some of the questions are designed to get you thinking about a subject.

You may already know some things about the subject. If this is the case, you can build on what you already know. You may know nothing about the subject. In this case, the learning process will require greater focus on your part.

Every even page contains information that supports the text. Feel free to add information or customize that information. There is also plenty of room on the pages of text for you to make notes or jot down key thoughts as you read.

At times you will be asked to use materials that you are currently studying. By stopping and practicing, the learning process will build at an increasing rate. The more you learn to learn, the faster you will be able to learn any subject.

Although the book has you answering, writing, and drawing, there may be other ways you learn better. Use what is best for you.

If you get stumped in this book or in the application of this program to another class, try a different approach to the same subject. You will learn several ways to approach the same subject in this book.

Before You Begin

- Look through the book
- Check out the Table of Contents for each module
- Review the questions at the beginning and end of each section
- Read the introduction to get an overview of the program
- Write down questions you may have before you even start

Find Your Place to Study

- Be comfortable, but not too relaxed
- No TV (You will learn why in the first module)
- If listening to music, there should be no words (You will learn what type of music is best for different types of study)
- Plan to study during the daylight hours if possible
- Plan to study in short cycles and review what you learn as you go

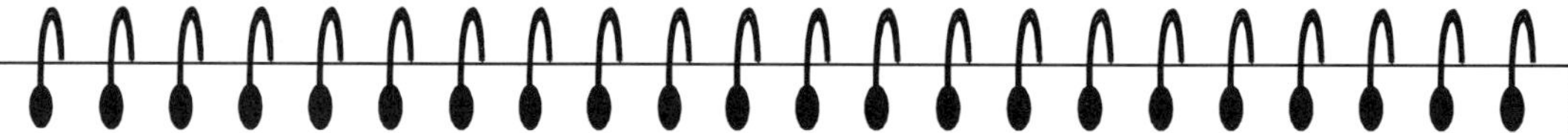

Daily Record

- ✓ Challenge
- ✓ Accept Others
- ✓ Learning Styles
- ✓ Organized Information
- ✓ Assimilated Knowledge
- ✓ Multiple Intelligences
- ✓ Showed I Know
- ✓ Met Plan

DAILY RECORD

To stay highly motivated and to recognize that you are succeeding, keep a Daily Learning Journal.

Every day, new things are learned that you do not always acknowledge. The Daily Learning Journal is a place where you can record every learning success as it occurs.

Record All Positives

Was I able to accept challenges as they came up?

Did I resist fighting or running away from another point of view?

Was I able to adapt with logic and reason?

Did I effectively use a new Learning Style?

Was I able to organize my thoughts from a Global perspective?

Did I organize the big picture into a Linear progression?

Was I able to attach or Assimilate new information with knowledge I already have?

Did I use multiple intelligences to show that I know?

Was I able to immediately use my new knowledge?

Did I meet my plan?

Answering all of these questions will be easy because they are all covered in this program.

Dendrites

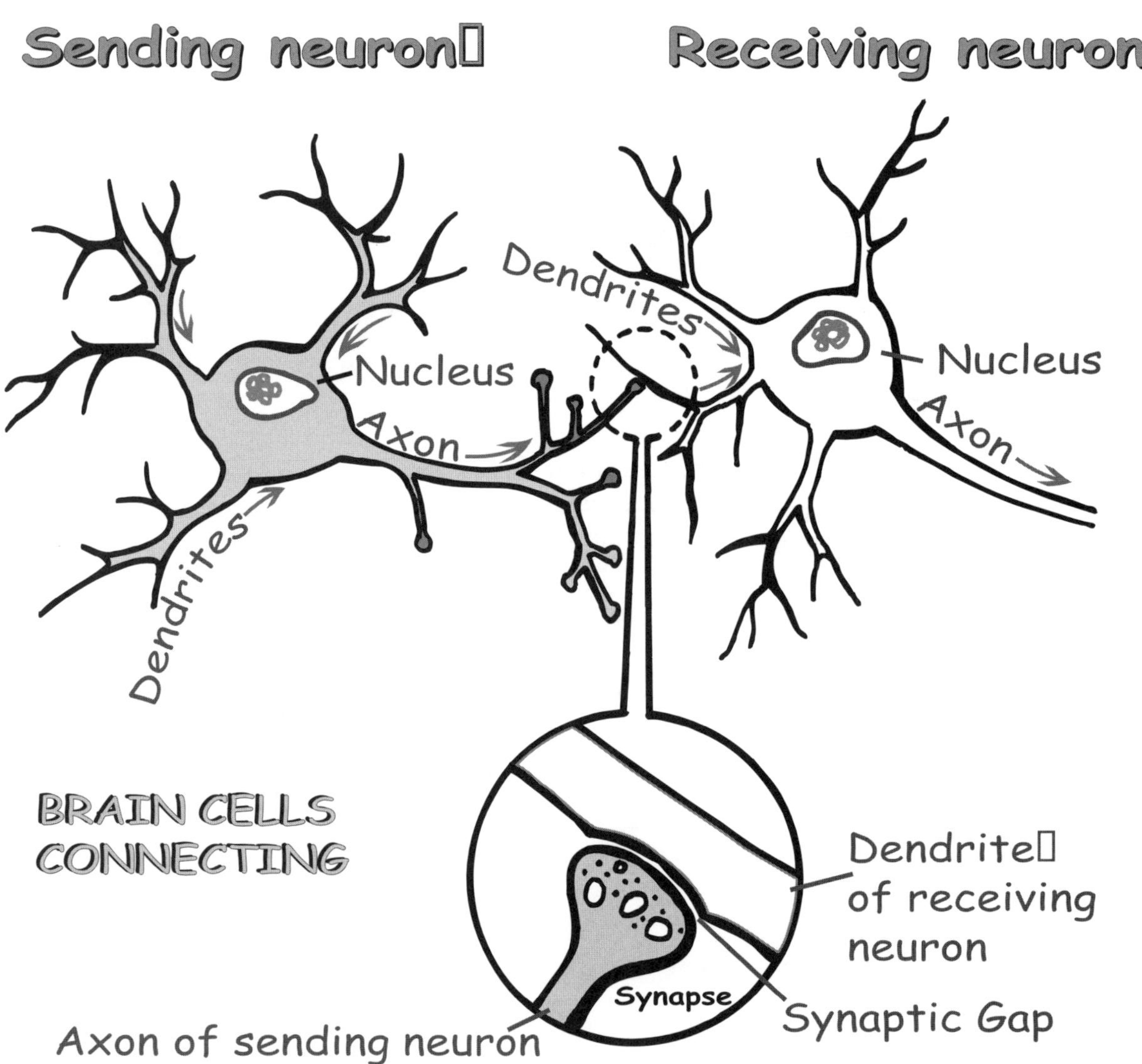

Sending neuron
Receiving neuron
Dendrites
Nucleus
Axon
Dendrites
Nucleus
Axon
Dendrites
BRAIN CELLS
CONNECTING
Dendrite
of receiving
neuron
Synapse
Synaptic Gap
Axon of sending neuron

LEARNING NATURALLY

From the beginning of life until the end, your life grows through learning.

You are able to do this by bringing information in through the five senses. Everyone learns by seeing, hearing, doing, tasting and smelling. The mind then organizes the information and the brain "accommodates" and makes room for the new information.

Information is stored, but it is not readily available to the memory unless there is some meaning to the information. The brain does not automatically create meaning. This is where you, as the learner, need to understand the ability to consciously create meaning.

Once the real meaning has been created, a series of brain connections take place. This natural growth occurs in the complex network known as "Dendrites". The more connections that are made, related to specific information, the greater the chance of memory recall.

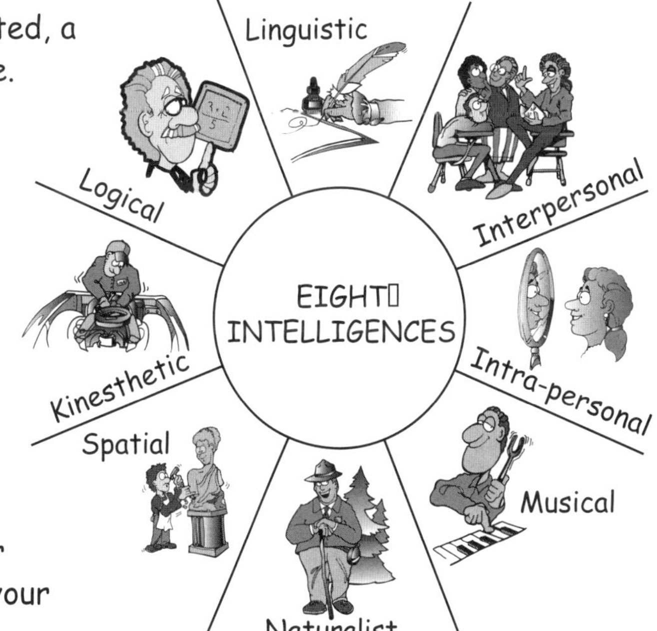

Once the information is in, you need to be able to share this knowledge with others. This is done with one or more of eight distinguishable skills or "intelligences" that are all built into your intellectual systems.

This is natural learning. The challenge is that natural learning is unique to each individual. You will also express what you have learned differently than other people in the class.

If you think
you can
or you think
you can't,
you are
probably right.

Henry Ford

You might also learn in a style that is different from the way the teacher teaches. If this is the case, you must learn to convert what is being taught to your own natural style.

FIRE-UP Your Learning will give you the tools you need to make that conversion. Everyone can learn naturally and generate amazing results.

Everyone is born with an equal and unique ability.

There are those who argue, "Yeah, what about Einstein or the kid who aces every test?" True, the Einstein's of the world use their brains in a more efficient and productive way than the "average" person. The kid who aces every test has also learned how to learn in a unique and efficient way.

More importantly, everyone can be a far better learner by understanding HOW to gain knowledge that is individually brain compatible. Everyone has the capacity to be a genius.

The aim of the FIRE-UP program is to allow you to understand HOW your particular, unique brain works and to give you the tools and techniques to expand and make use of your true potential.

F - Foundation

I - Intake Information

R - Real Meaning

E - Express Your Knowledge

U - Use Available Resources

P - Plan of Action

This course is only the beginning of your learning. When you have completed FIRE-UP you will have a simple six-step checklist of things that you should do to ensure good learning. The letters F-I-R-E-U-P represent these six steps. Explore the process and you will discover the key to your unique learning style.

Learn to use the FIRE-UP acronym as a reminder of the process to follow when tackling a learning project.

Learning Maps

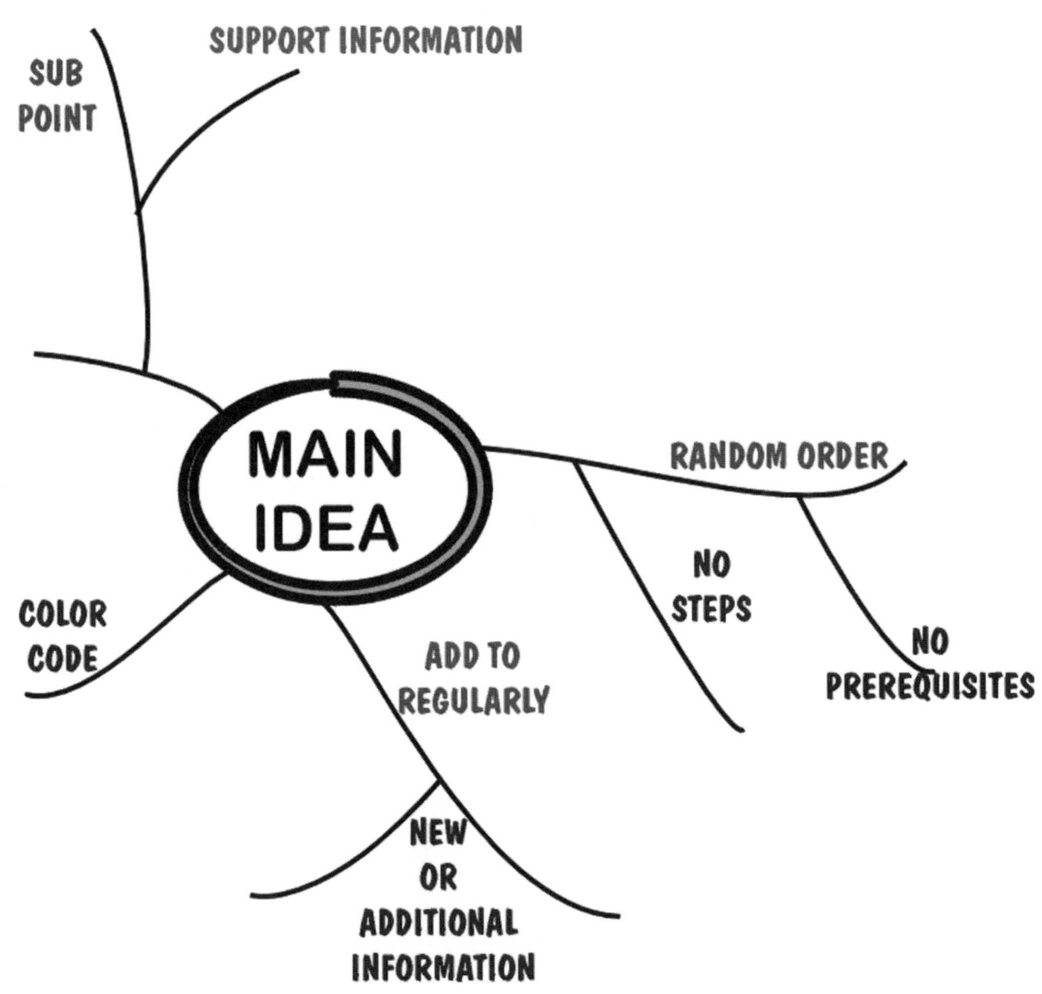

THE LEARNING MAP

If you prefer a totally logical, step-by-step approach, you can gain an overview of the program by following the Table of Contents.

An optional approach that is exceptionally powerful is the use of a Learning Map. Learning Maps are graphic representations of the information you are learning. You will be asked to create several Learning Maps throughout this program.

TO DO

ADD AS YOU GO

Learning Maps can be used while reading, planning, researching, listening to a lecture, listening to informational tapes or CDs, watching a demonstration, or any time you need to record information for easy recall.

There are two types of Learning Maps. One deals with recording random information and the other is used when there are specific steps involved in a procedure.

When randomly recording information, put the main idea in the center of the page. In a history class, for example, you may write World War II in the center. Branches from the center record key concepts related to the main topic. Branches off those branches will contain support information for the key concepts.

Use several colors to code the information being recorded.

Learning Maps

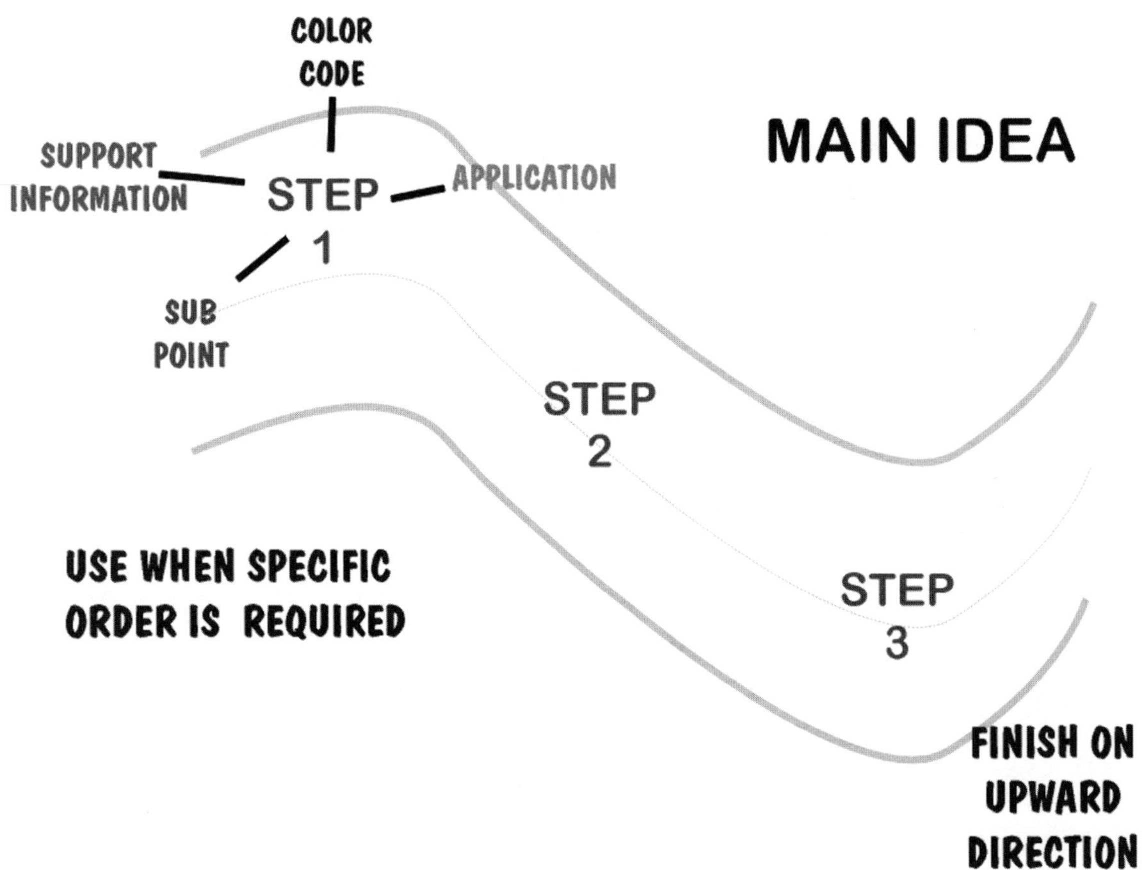

The second type of Learning Map is used when specific steps are required. In this case, draw a road map.

Title the page with the procedure. At the beginning of the trip through the procedure, list "step one" and continue from there. Branches or side-roads can be drawn off each step to record sub-steps or other supporting information.

Color is also a powerful way to store information in different parts of your brain. Color stimulates emotions associated with the materials being learned. Colors activate the right side of the brain (discussed in more detail later in the book).

Graphics, pictures and images will also enhance the learning map. Remember that the drawings you put on the map create more meaning for the subject you are studying. It does not have to be a work of art.

The more you practice the Learning Map techniques, the easier the process will become.

THIS
IS JUST
THE BEGINNING

On-Going Process

The completion of this course is just the beginning of your learning-for-life skill. The last module will culminate the development of a personalized Learning Plan of Action that you can apply to any learning situation. This will be your blueprint to ensure you learn in the most efficient way for your unique brain.

F·I·R·E-U·P

Intake Information

Foundations

Real Meaning

Express Your Knowledge

Use

Plan of Action

A GLOBAL LOOK AT EACH MODULE

Foundation - F

There are many ways that people remember. In Module One you will learn the FOUNDATION for many different techniques that can be used. The foundation lets you know why the information you are learning can be easily recalled when needed.

As more foundational information is made available, return to your Learning Map to build on what you already know.

Intake Information - I

In Module Two, you will discover your preferred style that allows you to INTAKE INFORMATION through visual, auditory or kinesthetic (sense of touch) channels.
Depending on what is being learned, the sense of taste (gustatory) and smell (olfactory) can be added to the learning style list.

No learner uses only one of these channels. After completing the "Intake Information" module, you will have discovered your main "intake style". You will also understand how to use all of the other styles to learn faster and easier.

Real Meaning - R

Module Three gives you the opportunity to create REAL MEANING for the new information you just took in. This is done through a process called "Assimilation".

Express Your Knowledge - E

Module Four gives you an opportunity to EXPRESS YOUR newly found KNOWLEDGE to someone else. When you show-you-know, it builds self-confidence. When you start to show you know and then realize you really do not know, back up. Take the information in using a different learning style or assimilation process.

You will express what you know through your intelligences. There are eight distinct intelligences that are used to comprehend information to the point that the information is easily discussed with others.

Foundations

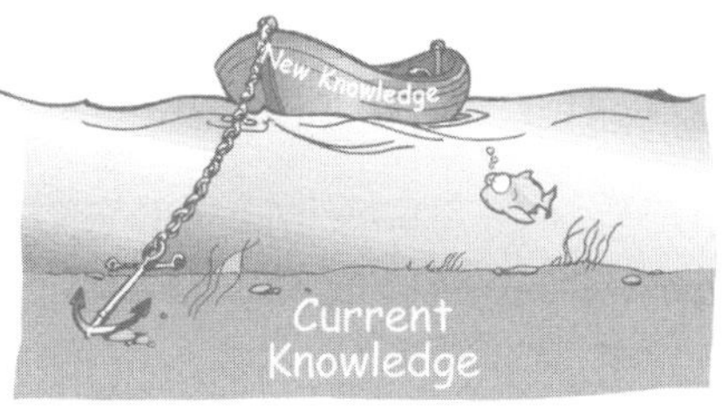

F·I·R·E-U·P

Express
Your
Knowledge

Plan
of Action

Module Five allows you to USE your newly found knowledge in different ways. You will also learn to use other people and resources to enhance the overall process.

Use Available Resources - U

Planning your learning is covered in Module Six. The PLAN OF ACTION will be based on all you have applied to this point. At the end of your course, a Learning Map will form the basis of your personalized Learning Plan of Action.

Plan - P

What questions, if any, do I have so far?

____

____

Instead of FIRE-UP, can I create another name to describe the learning process?

____

____

Is there anything additional that I would like to know about how to learn?

____

____

If yes, where could I research this information?

____

____

FOUNDATIONS

MODULE 1

Foundations

Intake Information

Real Meaning

Express Your Knowledge

Use Available Resources

Plan of Action

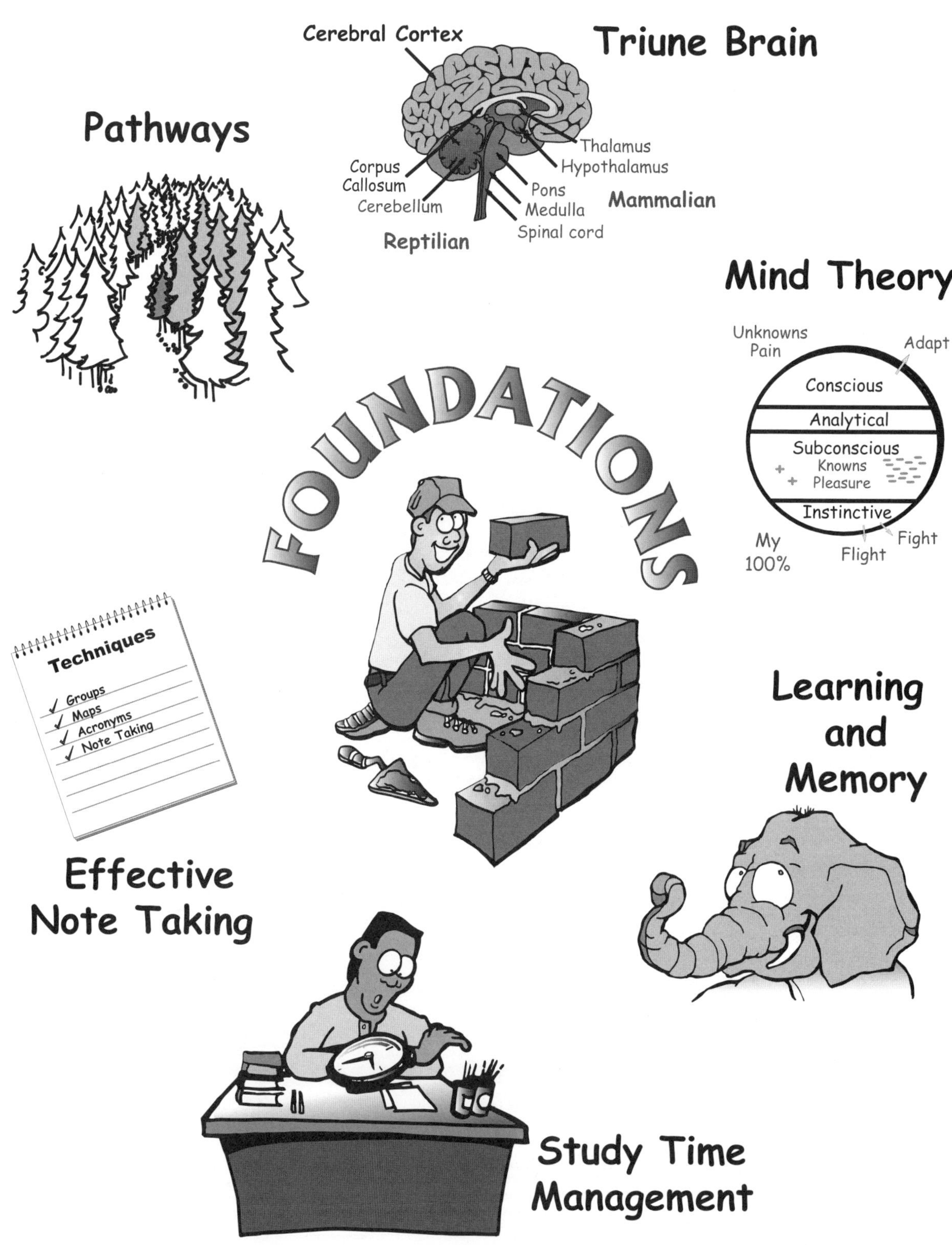
Triune Brain
Cerebral Cortex
Thalamus
Hypothalamus
Corpus
Callosum
Cerebellum
Pons
Medulla
Spinal cord
Mammalian
Reptilian
Pathways
Mind Theory
Unknowns
Pain
Adapt
Conscious
Analytical
Subconscious
Knowns
Pleasure
Instinctive
My
100%
Flight
Fight
FOUNDATIONS
Techniques
Groups
Maps
Acronyms
Note Taking
Learning
and
Memory
Effective
Note Taking
Study Time
Management

MODULE 1

F - FOUNDATIONS

Building Blocks Of This Module 25

The Methodology 25

Pathways In The Brain 29

Exercise = Growth 29

The Triune Brain Theory 31

Three Brains in One 31

Learning and Memory Implications 33

- The Mind 37
- The Conscious Mind 39
- The Analytical Mind 41
- The Subconscious Mind 57
- The Instinctive Mind 65

Memory 67

- Memory Movement 73
- Memories Can Be Trained 79
- Concentration 81

Study Time Management 85

Studying Text Books 93

- Effective Note Taking During Lectures 99
- Techniques for Taking Notes 111
- Learning Maps 111

Combining Charts 119

Summary - Module 1 121

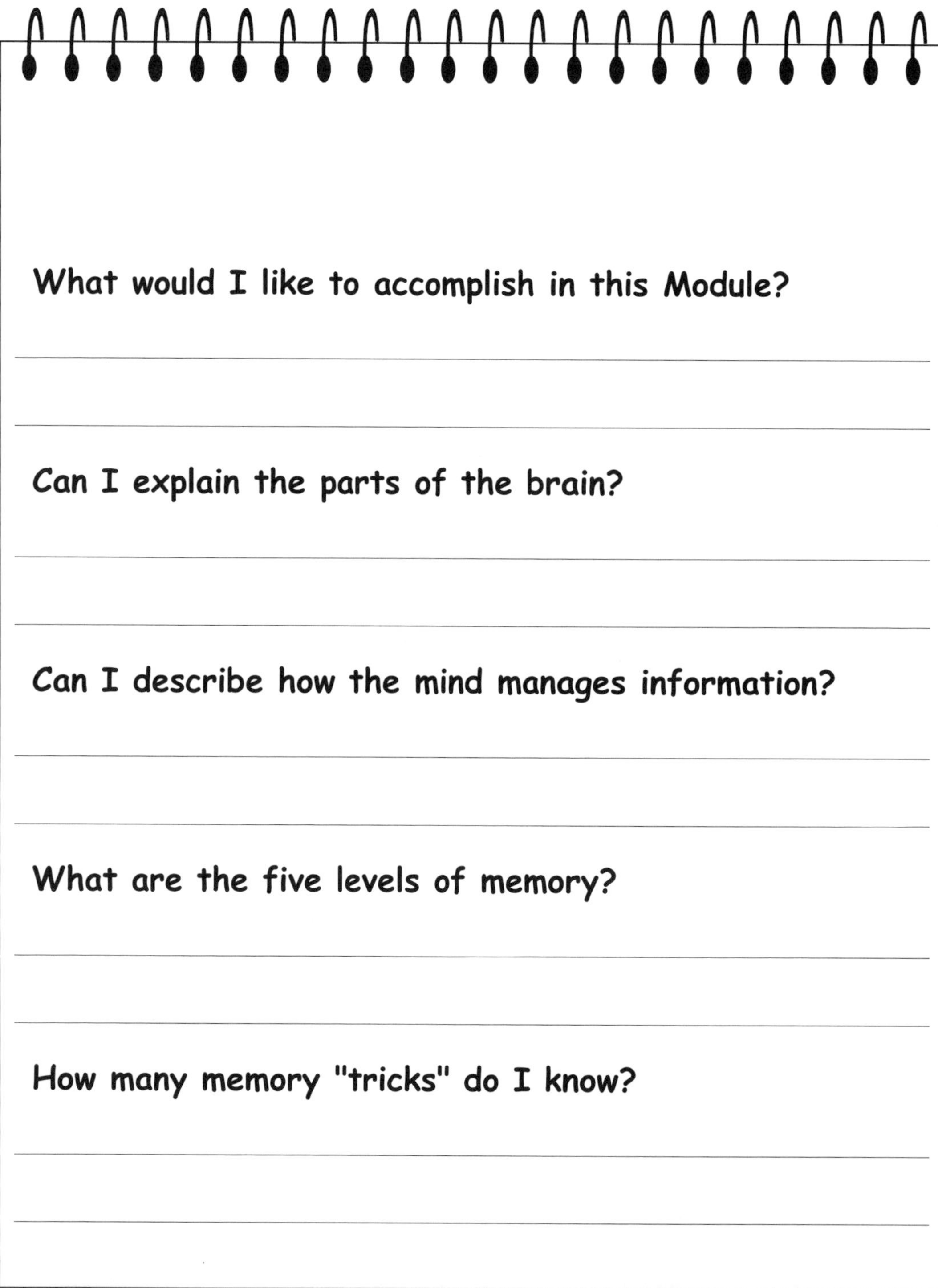

What would I like to accomplish in this Module?
Can I explain the parts of the brain?
Can I describe how the mind manages information?
What are the five levels of memory?
How many memory "tricks" do I know?

F - FOUNDATIONS

BUILDING BLOCKS OF THIS MODULE:

- **Accelerated Learning**
- **Your Brain**
- **Your Mind**
- **Your Memory**

Each person has the necessary components to be a great learner. All that is necessary is to find out how to make the most of these natural, inborn talents and attributes. As a result of life experiences, self-preservation barriers have been erected that inhibit learning. In this Module, therefore, you will address how to remove these barriers or turn them into stepping-stones in the quest to be a better learner.

THE METHODOLOGY

The Accelerated Learning methodology is based on findings and research from Universities around the world. It represents a collection of the latest scientific discoveries in the fields of brain research, memory and psychology. The practical, user-friendly methods will have a dramatic and positive impact on your learning.

FIRE-UP Your Learning will allow you to select the learning tools that work with your natural personal strengths. The program will also allow you to develop your own successful strategies to make learning easier, faster and FUN.

TRY THIS:

1. Slump down in your chair
2. Sink your chin on your chest
3. Make your face look glum and depressed
4. Now, try to feel happy!

It's almost impossible!
Your mind, body and brain are inseparable.

Accelerated Learning is whole-brain and whole-body learning

The way you hold yourself, the expression on your face and the thoughts in your mind are all inter-linked. A person's demeanor reflects thoughts and those thoughts are mirrored in one's posture.

If all these elements work together, then it makes sense to involve all of them in your learning.

If you are not sure of a word or phrase as you read this book, stop to take time to look it up. If you do not have a dictionary handy, ask someone who might know. If no one is around who would know, write the word down and look it up later.

The Accelerated Learning methodology is often misunderstood. Many people think that it only means to "learn faster". In reality, Accelerated Learning is maximizing brain efficiency by using your natural talents.

Learning in a style that is compatible with the unique way your brain functions, will lead to better intake of information and better understanding. This natural approach will improve results and may speed learning, but quality learning is the primary consideration.

TRY THIS:

Do another mind and body exercise.

1. Sit up straight in your chair, shoulders back and take a deep breath
2. Lift your chin slightly and give a little smile
3. Feel powerful and confident because that is what you are

PATHWAYS IN THE BRAIN

Imagine you are in a forest surrounded by trees. You need to get out from among the trees, but you look around and there seems to be no path. So, you head in a direction until you get to the edge of the forest.

INTAKE
=
LIGHT PATH

When you look back from the forest's edge, it is very difficult to see the path as the leaves and branches have sprung back into place.

If, however, you were to go back along this path a few times it would soon become visible. Eventually, after some time of regular use, the path will be permanent and ready to use whenever needed.

REHEARSAL
=
NARROW PATH

In our brain, there is a similar chain of events. As we intake information, a light path is created. When we create meaning, the path becomes increasingly visible. The widest path is created when we try a new task, adjust to make the task easier, and practice the task several times. A permanent path is now created.

Exercise = Growth

APPLICATION
=
WIDE PATH

Muscles grow through exercise and regular use. They also wither with non-use. The human brain is much like a muscle in that it too thrives on being used. It grows by being stretched.

By using and challenging your brain, more brain cells start talking to one another. As the brain cells communicate, new networks are formed through "synaptic" connections. Branches or "dendrites" from active cells will grow or split to be able to network with new cells. Since the new cells already have a set of information, knowledge crosses over. As information is shared, cells grow. The cycle begins again.

Dr. Paul MacLean's Triune Brain Theory

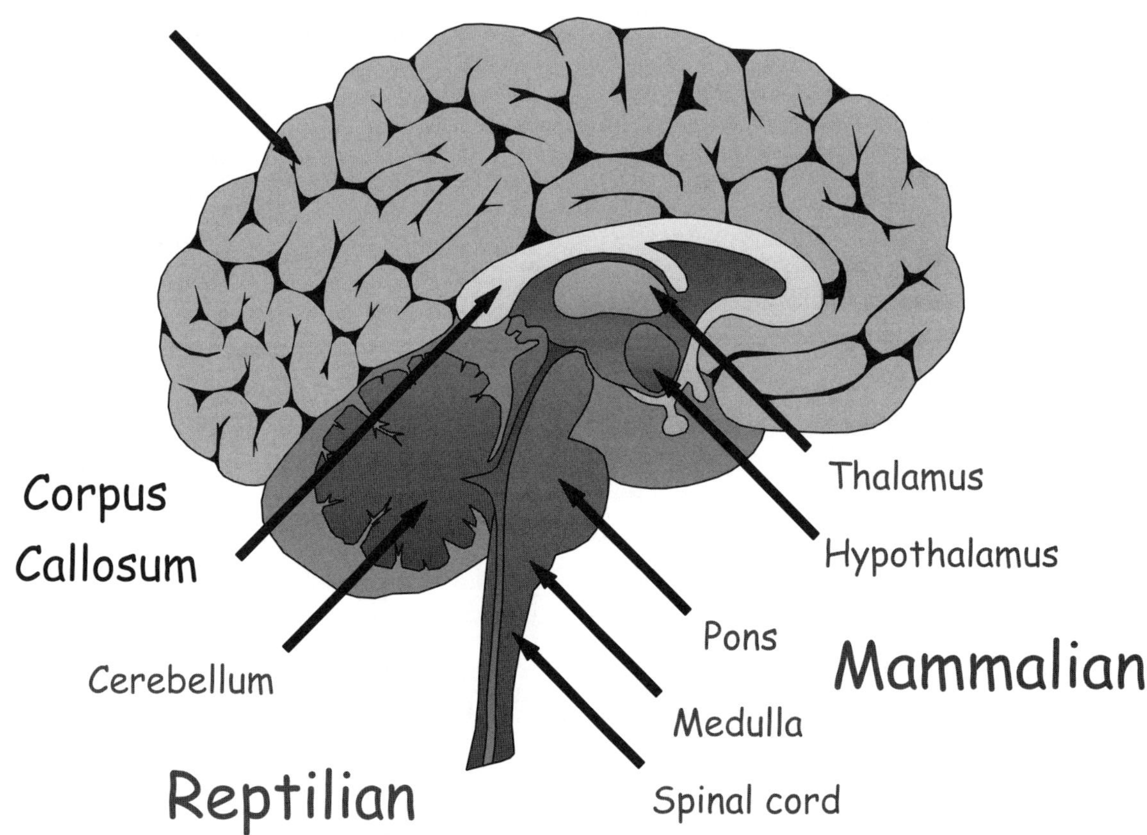

THE TRIUNE BRAIN THEORY

Three Brains in One

The human animal has been created with a unique brain structure. According to Dr. Paul MacLean, everyone possesses three distinct brains in one. Although these brains are overlapping, each has specific functions and implications for learning. The three areas are: the Reptilian Brain, the Mammalian Brain, and the Neo-Cortex.

> *(Please note that Dr. MacLean's theory has been advanced. The following adaptation of Dr. MacLean's theory, however, is an excellent metaphor in the learning process.)*

TO DO

> IF YOU ARE NOT SURE WHAT A WORD MEANS, DO SOMETHING ABOUT IT.
>
> - LOOK IT UP NOW.
> - HIGHLIGHT IT OR WRITE IT DOWN TO LOOK UP LATER.
> - ASK SOMEONE WHO KNOWS

The brain stem, at the base of the brain, is where the brain connects to the spine. This part of the brain is called the Reptilian Brain. This area houses the control center, autonomic nervous system, for bodily functions such as heart rate and breathing. The Reptilian Brain is also responsible for how a person reacts to danger or threats; e.g. fight or flight.

The brain extends from the Reptilian Brain into the Mammalian Brain. Contained in the Mammalian Brain is the need for family, social order, and belonging. Within the Mammalian Brain is the Limbic System. Various parts of the Limbic System are associated with emotions and memory.

Covering the Mammalian Brain is the Neo-Cortex. The Neo-Cortex allows individuals to think logically and with reason. Additionally, the Cerebral Cortex gives **human** animals the ability to think in the abstract.

Logical reason, abstract thinking and speaking are just a few brain-related functions that separate humans from all other animals.

Learning and Memory Implications

LEARNING AND MEMORY IMPLICATIONS

The Reptilian Brain is designed to act or react automatically without planning. This portion of the brain provides protection from physical assault or harm. When the Reptilian Brain is in control, survival overrides logic and reason. Learning is limited to issues related to continuing existence.

REPTILIAN BRAIN

Many people experience this reaction in examinations. The overload in the brain caused by fear or anxiety causes the reasoning brain to shut down. Have you ever taken a test and you just cannot get the answers? As soon as the test is over and you walk out of the classroom, the answers just pop into your mind.

MAMMALIAN BRAIN

The Mammalian Brain, sometimes called the Midbrain, influences the emotional aspect of learning. Research evidence shows the emotions generated in the Limbic System aid in the establishment of long-term memory.

NEO-CORTEX

Strong emotions are associated with a person's most vivid memories. There is a tendency to remember the highest highs and the lowest lows. The "outrageous" factors are clear, but all other memories are fuzzy or not as readily available.

The emotional factor can be utilized by incorporating positive emotions to enhance the learning process. Positive emotions are engaged through the use of drama, enthusiasm, creative controversy, and team projects.

REPTILIAN BRAIN - THE BODY GUARD

Protects us from physical harm

Reacts immediately

Manages the Physical World

LIMBIC BRAIN - THE REGULATOR

Regulates

- Immune System
- Hormones
- Sleep

Manages the Emotional World

NEO-CORTEX - THE THINKING CAP

Works with logic

Responds through reasonable thought

Manages the Creative World

The Neo-Cortex is the part of the brain that combines several pieces of information to create new information. The same words, for example, can be used to create a completely different meaning. Poems, songs, ideas, stories, or any creative problem solving is a result of the Cerebral Cortex bringing everything together.

The Neo-Cortex takes learning to a higher level when application of the newly found knowledge is exercised. A high school student, for example, can develop a science project that revolutionizes a certain technology. Someone about to retire can create an innovative application of a current program by blending a program used forty years ago.

Research indicates that energy moves from the brain's base (Reptilian Brain) through the emotional center (Mammalian Brain) to the top, front part of the brain (Frontal Lobe of the Neo-Cortex).

This means that when you are preparing to learn, you should be physically comfortable. Temperature, lighting and the study area should all satisfy the Reptilian Brain. You should go into the learning with a positive attitude to satisfy the emotional center of the brain. When the first two parts of the brain are happy, the thinking brain can work its magic.

How you approach your studies or a problem can also make a difference. If you look at something and say "What's wrong with this?" you will probably be negative. On the other hand, if you approach a situation with the attitude that there is a solution, your brain will work on creative solutions. The question is, "How can I improve this?" Do not focus on what you do not have, instead maximize what you do have.

Mind Theory

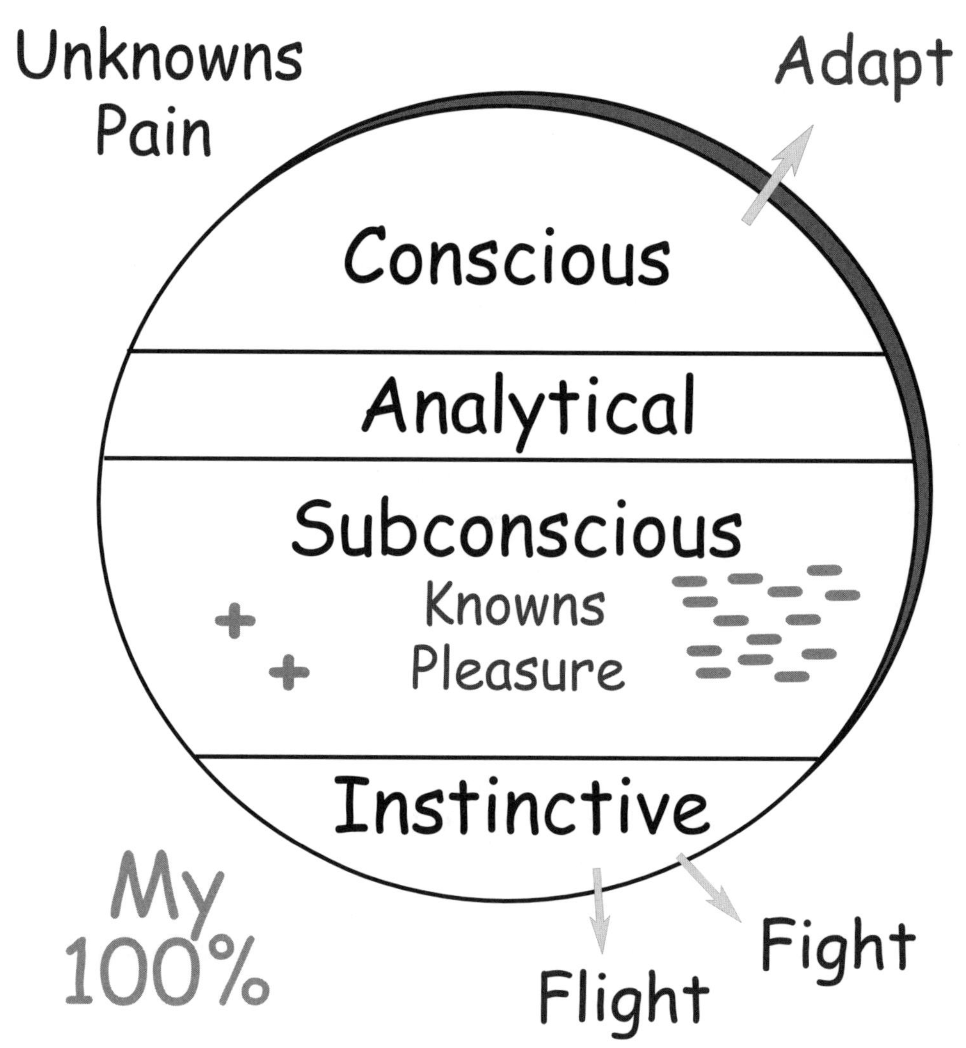
Unknowns
Pain
Adapt
Conscious
Analytical
Subconscious
Knowns
Pleasure
Instinctive
My
100%
Flight
Fight

THE MIND

Intermingled somewhere in the brain is the mind. From the beginning of civilization, people have attempted to explain what the mind is. The following information combines many theories that look at the "normal" mind. Abnormal psychology (bipolar, paranoia, schizophrenia, etc.) will not be explored.

The mind is made up of four key divisions:

The Conscious Mind

This is the highest degree of alertness or awareness.

The Analytical Mind

The Analytical Mind contains the "boxes" in which people live. Paradigms (see page 48), prejudices, and preferences help people decide what is acceptable and what should be rejected.

The Subconscious Mind

As an example, the Corpus Callosum, the part of the brain that connects the right and left hemispheres of the brain, can manage approximately 100 million bits of information per second. When watching TV, the signal is coming onto the screen between 16 and 128 bits per second.

The brain wins.

The Instinctive Mind

This is the area of the mind that protects a person's ego from verbal assaults. The Reptilian Brain is responsible for the physical attacks.

These four areas of the mind will be explored in terms of learning and memory.

The Conscious Mind is:

- AWARE
- ALERT
- INTENTIONAL
- DETERMINED

The Conscious Mind

The Conscious Mind deals mainly with a broad range of mental behaviors that include awareness, thinking, reasoning, and judgment. These are collectively known as cognition. The Conscious Mind can be the ultimate decision maker.

All of the other minds will, in different ways, influence the decision maker. The conscious mind, however, can override any of the other influences. The problem is that we do not always allow the Conscious Mind to be in control. Sometimes, for example, what is being taught might attack your personal belief system. The Analytical Mind considers and then rejects the information. The Instinctive Mind, recognizing the attack, protects against the perceived attack with a Fight-Flight Mechanism.

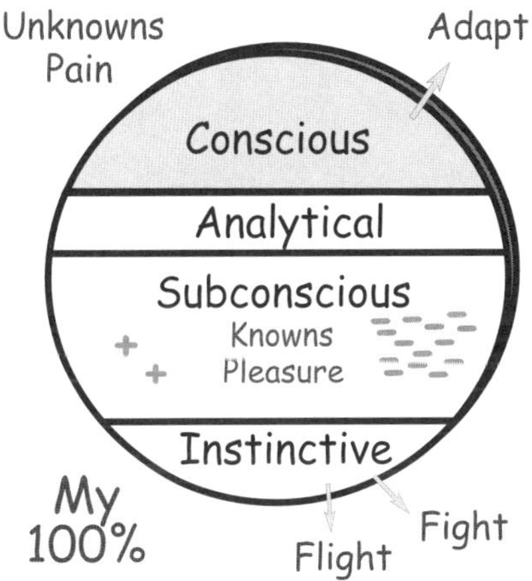

The Conscious Mind can stop the negative cycle by telling the Analytical Mind to re-frame the information. Analyze the other person's point of view. Why does that person think that way? What is it that I know that might be able to influence the way they think? How best can I communicate the differences in a solutions-oriented way? Do I care?

There is a buffer in this conflict between the Conscious Mind and the Subconscious Mind: the Analytical Mind.

Paradigms are a person's current models or examples.

A **preference** is a choice that is personally more desirable than another choice.

Prejudices are preconceived preferences or judgments made before the facts are established.

The Analytical Mind

The purpose of the Analytical Mind is to filter information between the Subconscious Mind and the Conscious Mind.

The Analytical Mind houses paradigms, prejudices and preferences. Paradigms are a person's current models or examples. A preference is a choice that is personally more desirable than another choice. Prejudices are preconceived preferences or judgments made before the facts are established.

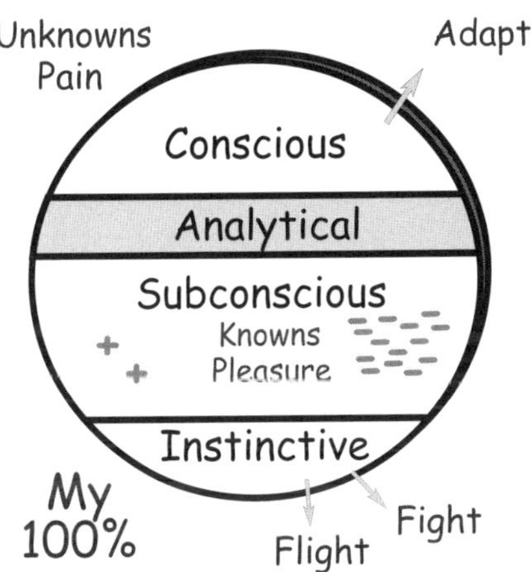

Once established in the Analytical Mind, these become the standards by which we compare and contrast everything we experience. There is good news and bad news about the process.

The good news is that the Analytical Mind prevents people from over-extending their individual capabilities. Basically, it keeps us from doing something really stupid. There are fences that go up to protect us from mental or physical injury. This allows us to work in an area that is secure. (NOTE: Alcohol and other drugs break down the fences and the protection they provide.)

The secure area is sometimes referred to as the "Comfort Zone".

Comfort Zone

The bad news is that the fences that protect us can also prevent exploration of new worlds of opportunity. Since the fences are at the edge of perceived capabilities, an individual will have a tendency not to attempt something that could create an "Unknown" environment. There are those who may go to the fence and peer through with hope and aspirations, but then quietly retreat back to the Comfort Zone.

The retreat back into the comfort zone is what is called a "rut". The definition of a "rut" is a grave with the ends kicked out. When people are in a rut, those people spend so much time looking at the dirt all around that they forget to look up to see all of the possibilities outside the rut. People in a rut tend to be slow to accept the new or innovative.

Caution is a positive attribute, but too much caution will restrict connectivity between brain cells and limit growth experiences. In any learning environment, the learner must be willing to be actively involved in the learning experience.

Imagine yourself in a study group with six other students. The group turns to you to explain part of a novel you have just read. Because you enjoyed the novel and knew the information as well, you took about fifteen minutes and reviewed the materials with the group. You were in your Comfort Zone with that material.

Now take the same knowledge you have with the novel and the same comfort level with the materials. This time the Principal of the school has asked you to present the same fifteen-minute overview to an assembly of 600 students in the auditorium. You might not be as comfortable as you were with the study group.

Analytical Mind

Comfort Zone

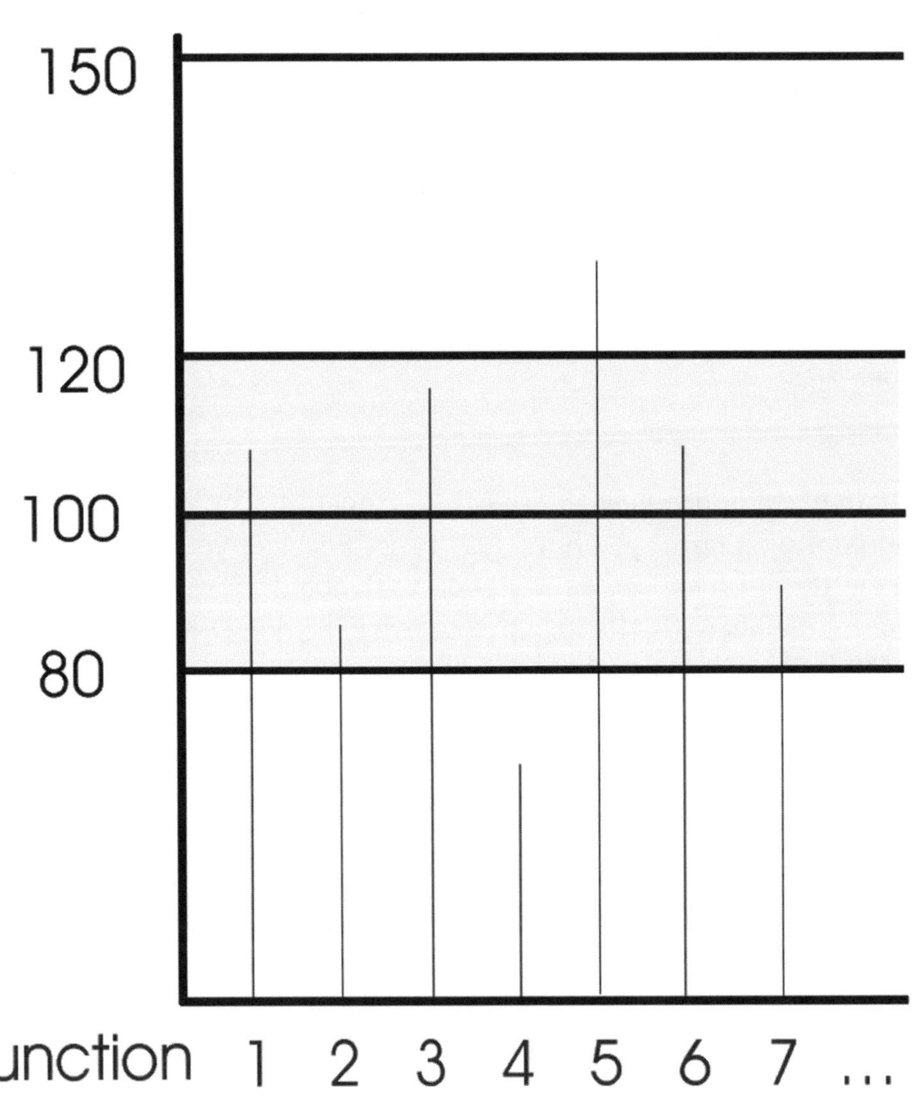

Why? You know the material. You have explained it before. The answer is Comfort Zone. Six hundred students in a huge auditorium with a microphone and spotlights on you, might be out of your Comfort Zone.

On the other hand, some people reading this may be saying, "What? I only get fifteen minutes?" For some, the second scenario is still within the Comfort Zone.

There are many books out there that warn of danger in the Comfort Zone. There is no danger in the Comfort Zone; there is comfort in the Comfort Zone. That is why it is called "comfort" zone. The problem is that the Comfort Zone sometimes becomes a rut.

> The objective in learning is to expand the Comfort Zone. Do not leap over the fences that are designed to protect you. Instead, push the fences out to give yourself more room for growth.

If you plant a tree in a field with no restriction, the tree will grow to its greatest capacity. On the other hand, if you plant a tree in a box, the roots can only grow to the edge of the box. The tree will never reach its greatest capacity.

As one door of
knowledge opens,

other doors of
opportunity to learn
will also open

The same applies to you. If your box is too narrow, build a bigger box. If your Comfort Zone is making a presentation to six people you know well, present the same information to six people you do not know well. Then present to a classroom of people. Then present to forty people. Eventually, it will not matter if you are presenting to six or six thousand. Your Comfort Zone will have expanded.

As you learn more, the Analytical Mind has a greater opportunity to compare and contrast new information coming in. The more you learn, the more you will be able to learn.

How do you eat an elephant?

Answer: One bite at a time.

OVERWHELMING SITUATIONS AND LEARNED DEFEAT

The Analytical Mind also looks at the size of the situation or project. If the project appears to be too large, the Analytical Mind will say, "You will never get this done. So, don't even try."

When a project appears impossible, break the project into smaller pieces. Then prioritize the pieces. Even if the project does not get completed, the most important parts will be done first.

> BREAK THE PROJECT INTO SMALLER PIECES, THEN PRIORITIZE THE PIECES.

How do you eat an elephant? The answer: One bite at a time.

What does this mean to you as a learner?

People in general are very susceptible to what others say and think. Research suggests that we will hear seven to twenty negative comments for each positive one! The next time you watch the news or a Soap Opera, count the number of negatives to positives.

> WE ARE WHAT WE THINK WE ARE.

Even on the conservative side, the seven to one ratio can easily chip away at our self-confidence. Lack of confidence or self-esteem can prevent people from trying to stretch their boundaries and maximize potential. Acceptance of the negatives can limit the ability to learn.

The Analytical Mind can filter information

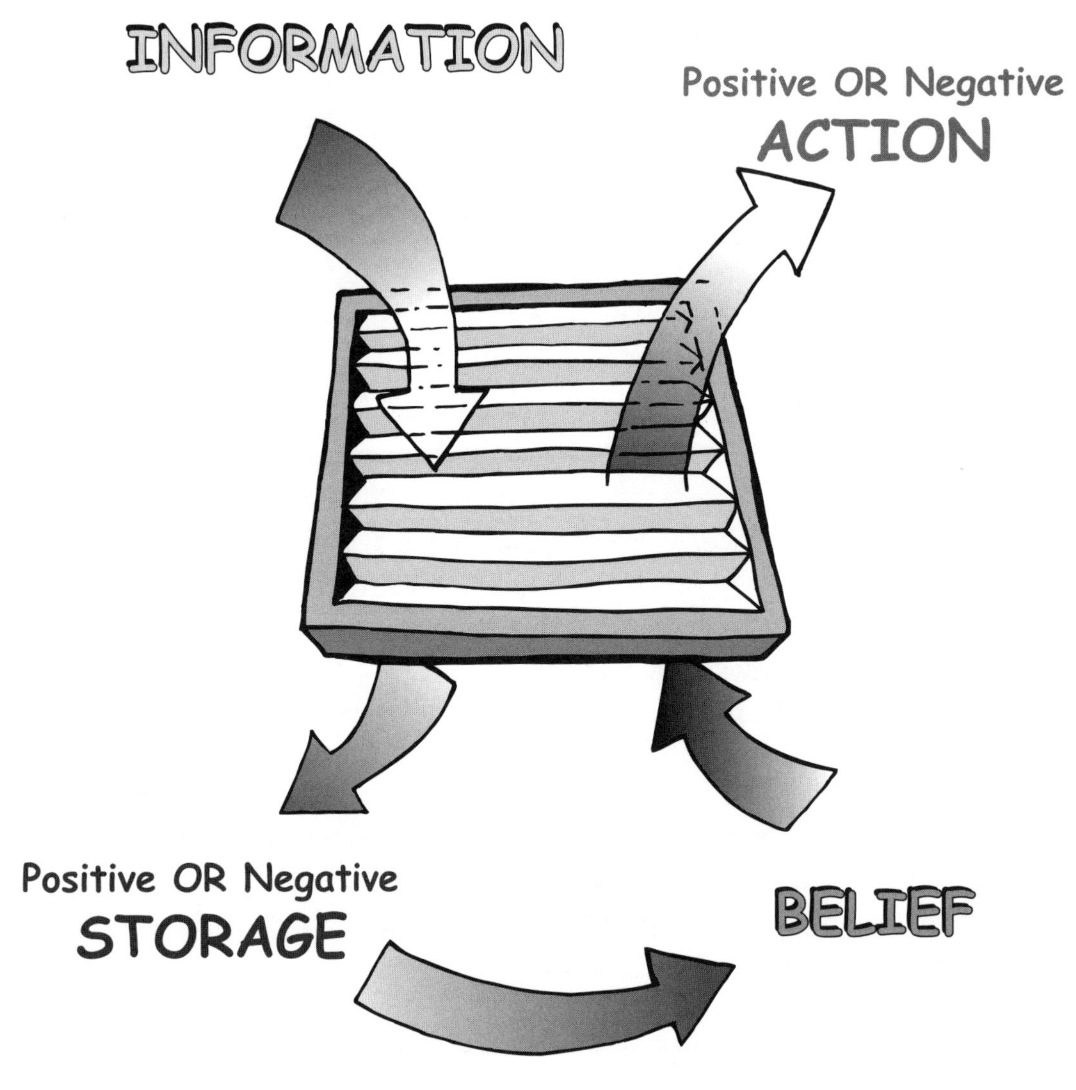

Negative self-talk is just as bad. The Analytical Mind can filter information from the Subconscious Mind into the Conscious Mind.

Mary is looking at a math problem. She tries to figure out the answer, but it keeps coming out wrong. Mary looks around at some of the other students who are finished with that problem and have moved on to the next one. Mary's Analytical Mind then tells Mary, "You are just not good at math".

Mary has a choice. She can either accept the Analytical Mind's point of view or she can override the Analytical Mind. "Yes I can get this. I will solve this problem."

The Analytical Mind can filter information

The good news is you can reprogram your mind to succeed.

You can address those negative influences, recognize them for what they are and move beyond them to be the person you were born to be. You can override your Analytical Mind and store positives by using the Conscious Mind to tell the Subconscious Mind what to store.

Positive Affirmations

Positive Affirmations

When developing positive affirmations, certain characteristics must be present.

1. The affirmations must be positive.

   Although this sounds obvious, the mind tends to store information in terms of symbols. Therefore, the mind may not catch all words in the affirmation.

   If a person wants to stop smoking, for example, the word "smoke" in an affirmation will create an image with which the mind will associate. "I will not smoke" is not a positive affirmation. The mind picks up the word "smoke" and ignores the "not".

   "I am in control of all of my habits" makes the affirmation more directly positive.

2. The positive affirmation must be in the present tense.

   "I AM" versus "I WILL BE". I "am" indicates that what you are doing is happening now. I "will" indicates that something will be done in the future. As you know, the future is never today.

   "I am good at math." "I understand Shakespeare." "Science is easy for me."

Affirmations

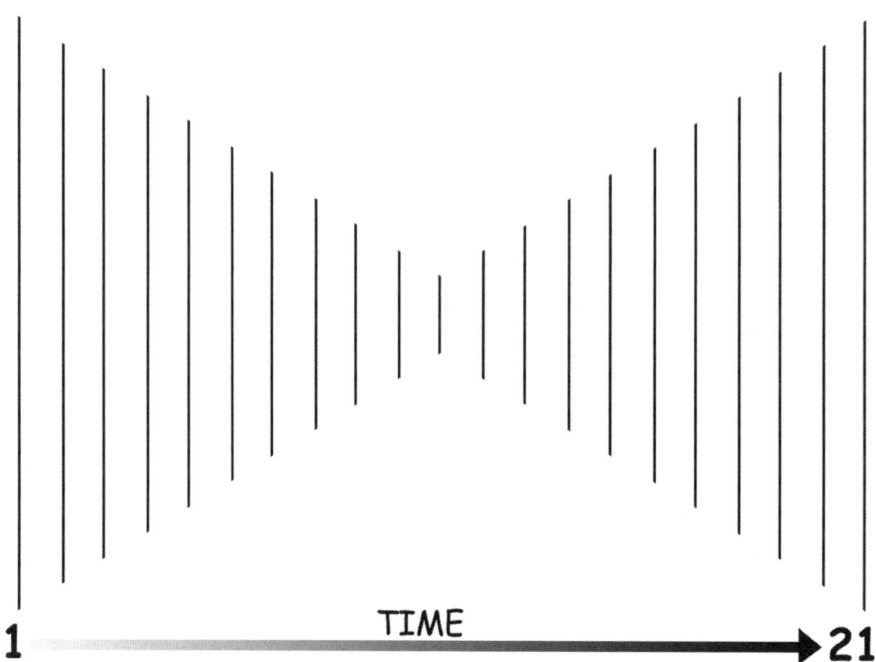

AFFIRMATIONS WORK OVER A PERIOD OF TIME.

- There is strong resistance in the beginning.
- There is neutral resistance in the middle.
- There is acceptance at the end.

Repeat the positive affirmation several times over 21 days.

3. **Positive affirmations must be constantly and consistently repeated.**

You are staring at a math problem that has you totally baffled. Everybody else seems to be getting it. You use a positive affirmation, "I am good at math". Your Analytical Mind says, "Who are you trying to fool? Face it. You are a loser at math."

The negative influence of the Analytical Mind must be overridden. Repeat the affirmation several times. Since your Subconscious Mind accepts what you tell it, the Subconscious Mind starts helping you out. "This problem is similar to one we solved earlier. Just substitute X for Y and there is the answer."

This may not work the first or second time, but with constant and consistent repetition, it will work.

Write out a positive affirmation for yourself.

____

____

____

____

____

____

____

Mind Theory

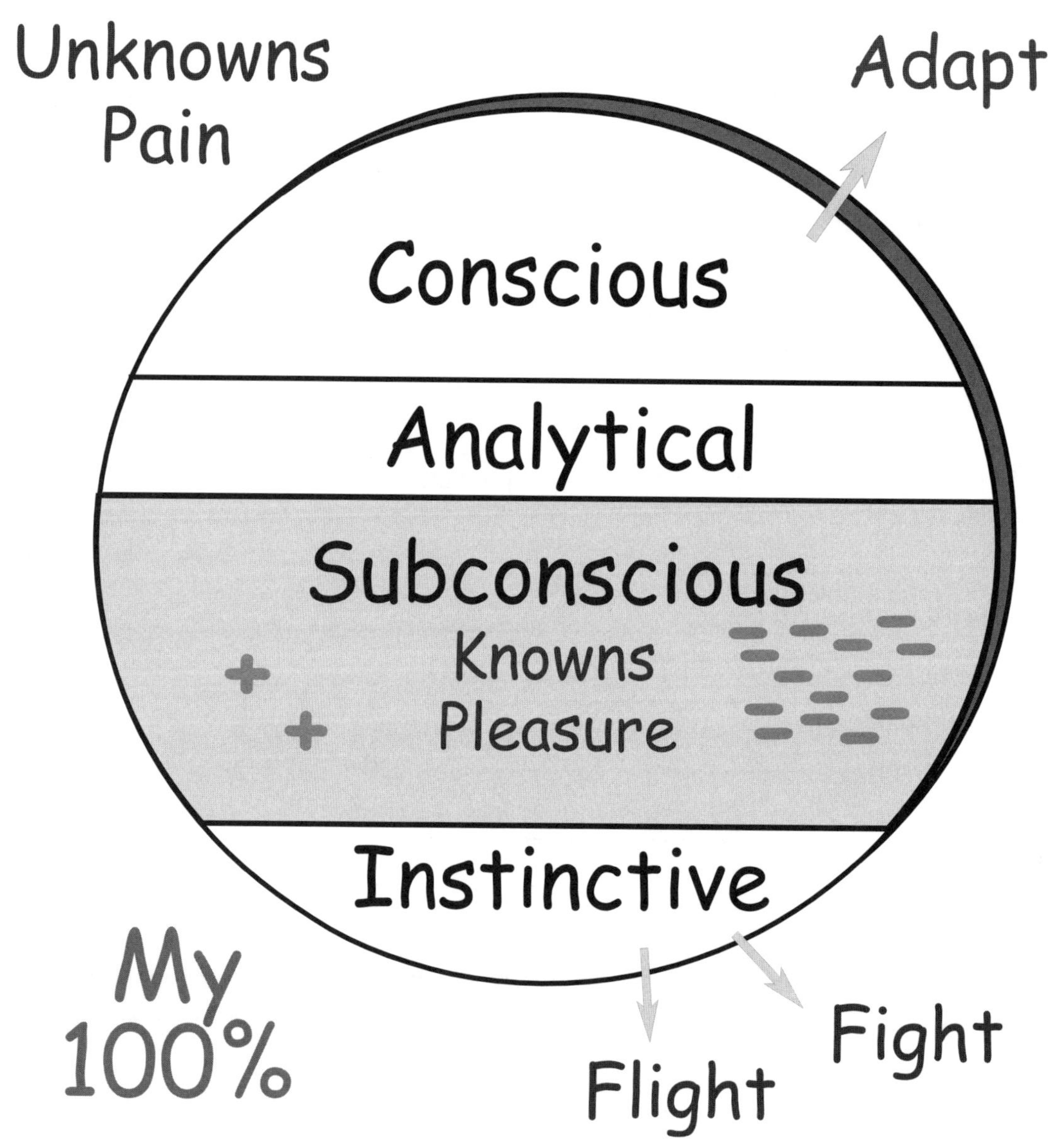
Unknowns
Pain
Adapt
Conscious
Analytical
Subconscious
Knowns
Pleasure
Instinctive
My
100%
Flight
Fight

The Subconscious Mind

Sometimes called the "Unconscious Mind", this mind has been a subject of controversy for thousands of years. Cave paintings have been discovered that depict dreams that cave dwellers "experienced". The ancient Egyptians believed in a "Mind's Eye" that gave them special insight. Greek philosophers speculated about the affect of the mind's invisible influence on various moral issues.

The location of the mind has even come into play. Descartes asked the question, "Is it possible that the mind is housed in the heart instead of the brain?"

At the beginning of the twentieth century, a flurry of theories focused the search to a more scientific approach. Freud developed theories that included subjects like the Ego, Id, Superego, repressed memory, and dream interpretation. Freud created a frenzy that led many other sophisticated scientists to explore this new world of the mind.

Technology has come a long way since then. Thought process can be "seen" through technology like the fMRI (Functional Magnetic Resolution Imaging) scans. Scientists know that different parts of the brain "light up" when people read, see, imagine, speak, and problem solve. The answers to many questions on the mind, however, have just created many more questions.

> THOUGHT PROCESS CAN BE "SEEN"

Comparisons

The focus in this text is on the Subconscious Mind in terms of learning, memory and general communication skills. The "broken brain" that causes abnormal behavior like schizophrenia or bipolar disorders will not be addressed.

As mentioned earlier, comparing a computer to the brain is like comparing a grain of sand to the beach. The Subconscious Mind, however, can be compared to the hard drive on a computer. The drive stores information in the form of symbols. Also, information is stored as it is recorded.

> COMPARING A COMPUTER TO THE BRAIN IS LIKE COMPARING A GRAIN OF SAND TO THE BEACH

The computer does not argue with the work, it just saves the work. If you typed a controversial term paper, the computer would not come back and argue with you, the writer, about the paper or its content. When you hit "save", the information is saved as is.

The difference between the computer and the Subconscious Mind is that the mind can never be shut off. Even when a person sleeps, the mind is processing, storing, rehearsing, and updating the current set of files stored.

The other key difference is that experiences cannot be erased or deleted. A person who has experienced a traumatic situation may have friends (or some professionals) who say, "You must forget about it and move on."

The reason that the advice is so difficult to accomplish is because the trauma cannot be forgotten (according to Freud, the trauma can only be repressed). The best that an individual can do is to consciously manage the event by controlling the emotions surrounding the event.

There are Positive Knowns and Negative Knowns

Knowns are pleasurable

Unknowns are painful

This is why people would rather stick with negative knowns than try something new

The Subconscious Mind stores KNOWNS

Everything that is experienced is stored. Unless there is some form of brain damage caused by a trauma, alcohol and other drugs, experiences are stored. Although some may argue this point, Psychiatrists, Psychologists and Hypnotists have been able to open memories that people have written off as lost. Levels of memory will be discussed later.

There are two types of "knowns". There are positive knowns and there are negative knowns. As mentioned earlier, a person gets hit with many more negatives than positives everyday.

Listening to music with negative messages may seem harmless at first glance. Listening to that same music over and over starts to cause layers of that message. Music with similar messages overlap and add to the layers of negativity.

Over a period of time those negatives can build up and become overwhelming. This is one of the reasons there are so many negative people in the world. The Conscious Mind can control the negatives and override their influence.

More importantly, the knowns are within the boundaries of the Comfort Zone. Outside the Comfort Zone is the cold, cruel world of "Unknowns". Unknowns are not comfortable and can create anxiety, fear and pain. Knowns, on the other hand, are pleasurable and comfortable. This is why many people would rather stick with a negative known than to try something new.

UNKNOWN
KNOWNS

Of course, trying something new is what learning is all about. The best way to limit the anxiety related with the unknown is preparation, associations and educated guesses.

Preparation forces the unknowns to be substituted with knowns. Preparation, in turn, generates greater confidence and willingness to push the limits of the Comfort Zone.

TO DO

COMPARE AND CONTRAST THE CURRENT SITUATION TO SIMILAR SITUATIONS

Associations compare and contrast the current situation to similar situations in the past. How was it handled then? Did it work or not? Why? How does this situation apply? It is difficult to conjure up illogical thoughts when conducting a logical examination of the circumstances.

Educated Guesses are attempts to eliminate unknowns through using the best options based on the current sets of knowledge. When the guess is made, the answer is right, wrong, or partially right. In any case, the learner now knows what works and what does not work. The learner knows what to study and can now focus on the information most appropriate to eliminate the unknowns.

Keep in mind that the Subconscious Mind needs to be told what to do. If the Analytical Mind is allowed to tell the Subconscious Mind to worry or give up, it will. If the Conscious Mind engages all of the information stored in the Subconscious Mind to solve problems and identify opportunity, it will.

Mind Theory

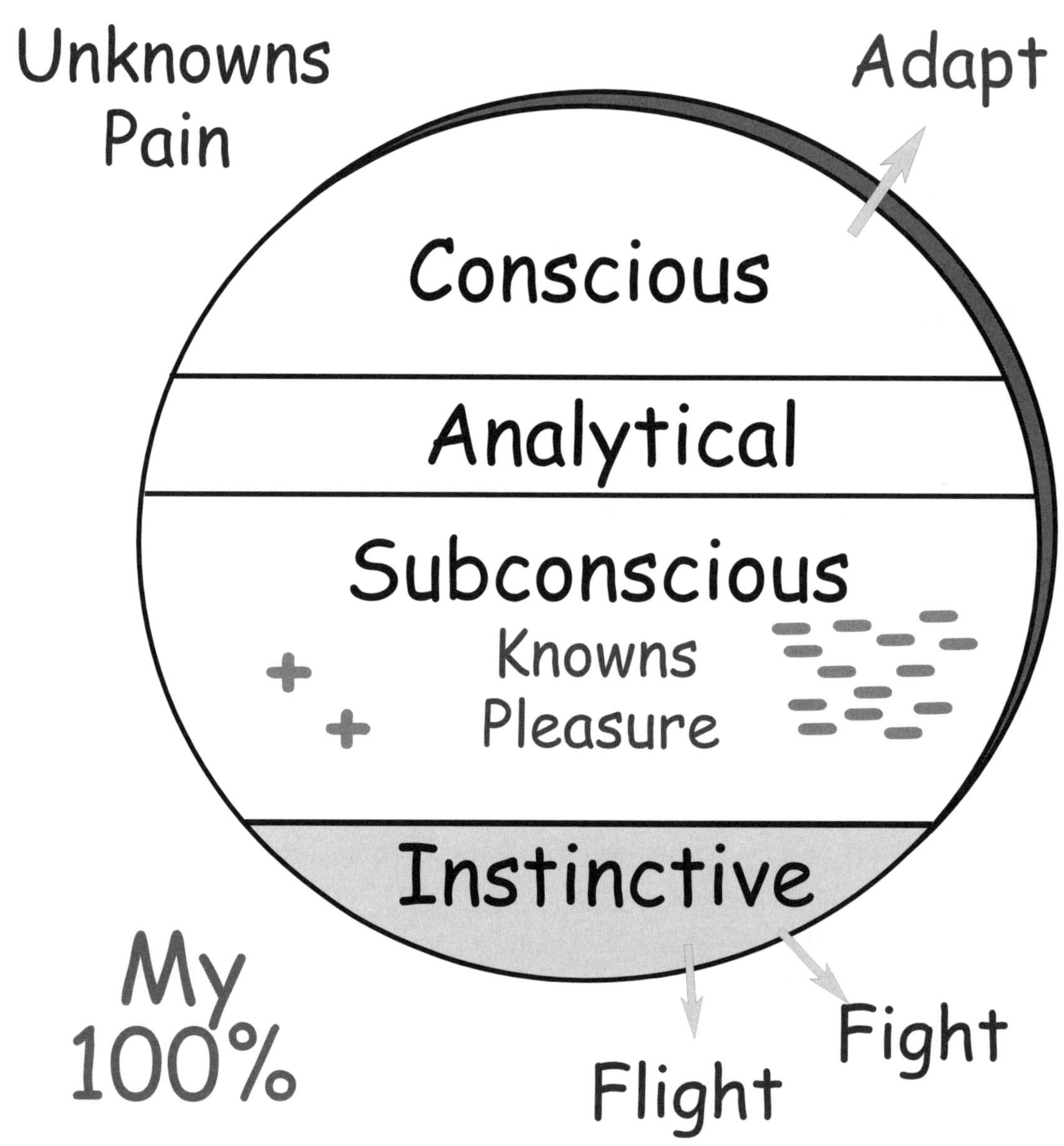

Unknowns
Pain
Adapt
Conscious
Analytical
Subconscious
Knowns
Pleasure
Instinctive
My
100%
Fight
Flight

The Instinctive Mind

The Instinctive Mind is the ego guard. Although no one knows exactly where the mind is, research seems to indicate that this "Instinctive Mind" protection mechanism is housed at the base of the spine (Reptilian Brain) and in parts of the complex Limbic System (Mammalian Brain) where emotions are activated.

FIGHT MECHANISM

Whereas the Reptilian Brain represents protection from physical harm, the Instinctive Mind generates protection from ego harm. It reacts instinctively in one of two ways: Fight or Flight.

The **fight mechanism** is a counter attack type of approach. There are even times when the Instinctive Mind uses a preemptive strike when it anticipates an ego assault. On the negative side, it is argumentative, belligerent, and sometimes violent. On the positive side, it is proactive and projects leadership.

The **flight mechanism** responds to the attacks by running away or trying to hide from the outside stressor. On the negative side is avoidance behavior and physical illness. In extreme cases, the result could be suicide. On the **positive side** is the fear that keeps people from danger, increased adrenaline flow, and the creation of a defensiveness that justifies an individual's actions.

FLIGHT MECHANISM

All four minds are working at the same time. **One may outweigh the other depending on the circumstance.**

Five Levels of Memory

Short-Term Immediate

Short-Term Working

Short-Term Intermediate

Long-Term Working

Long-Term Archive

MEMORY

Scientists are learning more and more about the brain and how information is stored and recalled. The discovery of several layers of memory have expanded short-term and long-term memory theory. The following description combines and simplifies three recent theories on memory.

There are five key areas of memory:

Short-Term Immediate

Short-Term Working

Short-Term Intermediate

Long-Term Working

Long-Term Archive

The **Short-Term Immediate** memory is where new information comes into the brain. In human beings versus other animals, this memory is housed in the frontal lobe of the Cerebral Cortex in the brain. The Short-Term Immediate memory can only manage about seven bits of information (plus or minus 2) before it transfers the information into the Working or Intermediate memories.

IT IS ESTIMATED THAT THE BRAIN CAN MANAGE APPROXIMATELY 100 MILLION BITS OF INFORMATION PER SECOND.

Memories

NOTES
HISTORY
Intermediate Memory
Short-term Working Memory

People are constantly receiving millions of bits of information per second. Knowing that the Corpus Callosum can manage 100 million bits per second, seven bits must be transferred instantaneously (nanoseconds).

The **Short-Term Working** memory is like a notebook that is open on your desk. It is being written in, read or otherwise doodled on. Most importantly, it is what is currently in focus.

> SHORT-TERM WORKING MEMORY IS WHAT IS CURRENTLY IN FOCUS

The **Short-Term Intermediate** memory is the notebook in a pile in the corner of the room. You can go get it if you need it, but right now it is just not important.

The Short-Term Intermediate memory is also like the "recycle bin" in your computer. When you clean up your active files, you send information to the recycle bin. The difference is that in a computer you can "empty" the recycle bin, but in the Short-Term Intermediate memory the information is always there.

At night, while sleeping, all of the short-term information gets downloaded into the long-term memories. Another decision needs to be made. Is this information I am going to need tomorrow or in the very near future? If the answer is yes, the information gets stored in the Long-Term Working memory. If the answer is no, the information gets archived.

Short-Term Memory downloads to the Long-Term Memory while sleeping

The **Long-Term Working** memory is knowledge needed for everyday use. You need to know where you live, what your telephone number is, and so on.

The **Long-Term Archive** memory is knowledge you are not currently using or will not be using for some time. Archived memory also piles up. More stuff gets piled on top of it making the originally archived memory difficult to retrieve.

SHORT-TERM INFORMATION GETS DOWNLOADED INTO THE LONG-TERM MEMORIES

It is like the stuff in the basement of a house. At first the basement was empty. Then box one got put in the corner. Eventually box two was stacked on top. Then three through five hundred were added. Box one is still there, but getting to box one would be difficult even if you remembered you had a box one.

The brain will open files with similar information

Memory Movement

The major difference between a basement or computer and the brain is that all of the knowledge stored is connected in some way. If you are working on a project on the computer and you type certain information in, no other files on the computer will automatically open with similar information. File one does not know what is in file two.

The brain, on the other hand, will open files with similar information. Imagine driving down the street and a song comes on that you have not heard for several years. All of a sudden, memories of events that occurred when you originally heard the song start to appear out of nowhere.

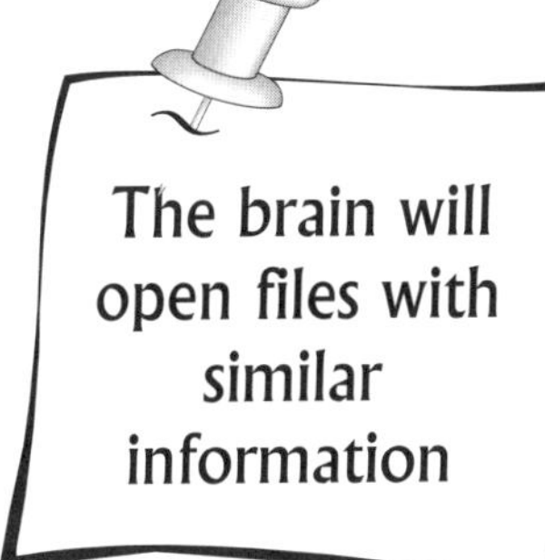

The music stimulated the Short-Term Immediate memory. The Short-Term Immediate memory sent a signal to the Long-Term Archive memory to open a file in the Short-Term Working memory. As soon as the song was over, the Short-Term-Working memory put that file in the Short-Term Intermediate memory. That night, while sleeping, the memory stimulated by the music gets put back in a box to be stored in the basement.

Declarative and Procedural Knowledge

Declarative

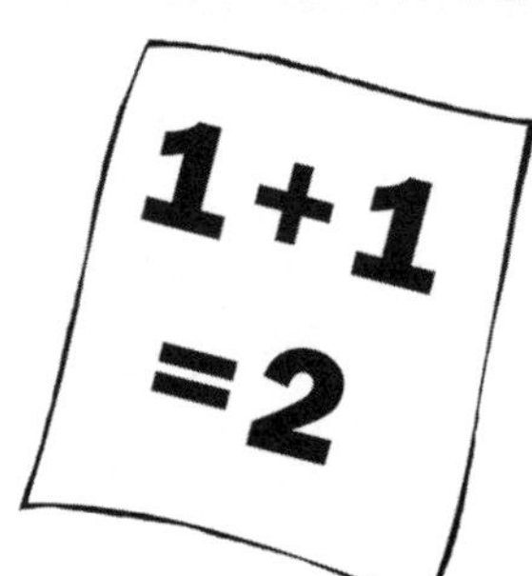

Procedural

You have one apple. A friend gives you one additional apple.

How many apples do you have?__________

How did you get the answer?

____

TYPES OF KNOWLEDGE:

Procedural and Declarative

By definition, Declarative Knowledge is information that is directly interpreted by or associated with other specific information. "Hola" in Spanish is "Hello" in English.

The definition of Procedural Knowledge is contextual utilization of information. You are in a hotel in Cancun, Mexico. While standing at the window admiring the beautiful beach, someone knocks at the door. Anticipating a Spanish speaker on the other side, you answer the door and say _______.

> PROCEDURAL KNOWLEDGE IS STORED IN A MANNER THAT CONNECTS MULTIPLE MEANINGFUL EVENTS

In other words, the declarative information will become part of a much larger picture or set of information. As the isolated piece of information is blended into the big picture, the declarative information becomes a meaningful addition.

It is much like creating a collage. Scattered about the table are many pictures and key words. By themselves, the individual pieces are basically meaningless. Once the individual pieces are placed on the paperboard and organized, connections between graphics and words start to form a larger, more meaningful picture. As new, isolated pieces (declarative information) are added to the overall collage, the piece now becomes part of the picture. This not only creates meaning for that piece, but it changes the overall meaning of the art.

Declarative and Procedural Knowledge

Now the collage becomes a storyboard (procedural). Any one piece can then stimulate recall of any other piece on the work.

"Hola" in the first context was declarative. If learning Spanish, a student could try to memorize this word with hundreds of others. Unfortunately, this type of rote memory will be short-lived because of two main reasons.

1. The word is meaningless. The word is not being stored in correlation with other associated events.

2. Recall of a word that is memorized in a declarative fashion is difficult. Because word 1 is associated only with word 2, it will require word 1 to generate recall of word 2.

Procedural Knowledge is stored in a manner that connects multiple meaningful events. In the second scenario, the word "Hola" is stored in a practical use situation. Meaning for the word can now be formed.

Secondly, "Hola" can now be recalled from many stimuli. A hotel in Cancun, beautiful beaches, and someone knocking at the door will have the ability to activate recall. The word learned will now be stored in a Long-Term Working memory for easier access.

Memories Can Be Trained

Cramming

Have you ever "crammed" for a test? You go to class the next morning and take the test. Ten minutes after the test is over, you know you could not take that test again without re-cramming.

The reason is that cramming generally includes memorizing Declarative Knowledge. Once the test is over, the mind does not need that information any longer because it is basically meaningless. Therefore, the Declarative Knowledge will be thrown in the basement with all of the other meaningless information.

Memories Can Be Trained

People who entertain us with their amazing memories have spent time developing storage and recall techniques. They have a strategy that works for them. Everyone can develop strategies that work. There are volumes written on memory techniques.

FIRE-UP is the overall process for bringing information in, organizing the information, storing it in a place easily accessible, and telling others what you know. There are additional techniques spread throughout the book that support the FIRE-UP process to exercise and strengthen your memory.

What do I do to concentrate when there are distractions all around?

Concentration

1. Find a place to study that will only be used for studying. This allows you to establish an environment with many study tools and limited distractions.

2. Control the noise level and the visual environment. Music will be discussed in more detail, but for now, music should be calming and contain no words when bringing information in. Different music can be played when being creative.

Avoid:

- Telephone
- Computer games
- Television
- People who want to talk about non-study subjects
- Junk food

Have:

- Plenty of light (indirect lighting is better than fluorescent lighting)
- Good ventilation
- Comfortable chair (but not too comfortable)
- Room to spread out your papers
- Water or fruit juice

Where is the best place for me to study?

3. Avoid getting too comfortable while studying. Being relaxed is fine, but being too relaxed allows your mind to wander and get distracted from the main goal.

4. Study during the day and early evening for maximum memory results. Avoid study times when there may be competing activities like band practice or a school athletic event.

5. Stop studying when fatigue sets in causing a lack of concentration. Take a break and perform a task that might move the studying forward, such as organizing research articles. Sometimes a five-minute walk around the block will rejuvenate your focus.

People remember more at the beginning and at the end of a learning session with retention dipping in between.

6. Keep a pad handy for thoughts or ideas that come to mind that are not related to what you are currently studying. Have several pages titled so the random thoughts can be organized. Page titles can include other subjects, a personal to-do list, and page for questions that you need to ask in class.

Time Management

STUDY TIME MANAGEMENT

1. Set SMART goals. (See "Plan of Action" which is the "P" in FIRE-UP.) The goals need to be targeted to the time currently available to study. This will make the goal attainable. Setting goals that are not attainable causes distress and breaks concentration.

2. Set study time based on the material that needs to be studied. Often, students set aside a fixed time during the day to study. Unfortunately, the material that needs to be studied may be more or less than that time. If the material requires more time, the study is not complete. If the material takes less time, the excess time is being wasted.

3. Be prepared to fill "down time". During the day there will be gaps of time between classes or events. Always keep study tools with you to take advantage of that time.

Create your own Flash Cards

Carry your "Learning Map" notebook

Carry a book that you need to read or review

Plan on meeting a study partner

Weekly Calender

Sunday

Monday *Classes - 9am and 2:30 pm*

Tuesday *Pop Quiz - Possible*

Wednesday *Paper Due*

Thursday *Chapter 5 - History Test*

Friday

Saturday

4. Keep a working calendar. You may think you will remember all assignments, but one or two may slip through the cracks. The calendar is also useful for scheduling study times throughout the day.

    - Set study time just before a class that requires discussion or that has many pop quizzes. The information will be fresh going into the class.

    - Maximize the daylight hours. Research shows that study during daylight hours is twenty percent more effective than hours after sunset.

    - Study immediately after classes that are mostly lecture. Create a learning map of the lecture. Review your lecture notes (see note taking).

5. Establish a study routine. If possible, study at the same time every day. If it is not possible to study at the same time everyday, set the same schedule for each day of the week. Monday, for example, may be first thing in the morning, Tuesday might be just before lunch break, and so on.

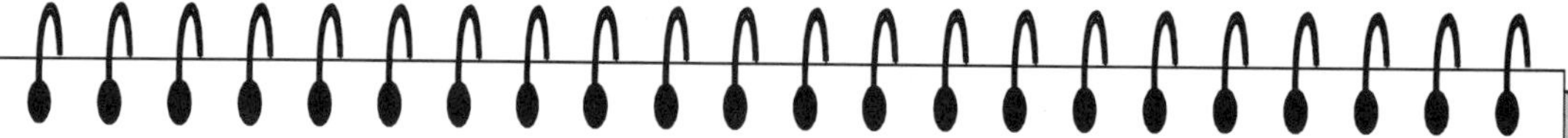

If you say,"I will do the project when I get around to it", go no further.

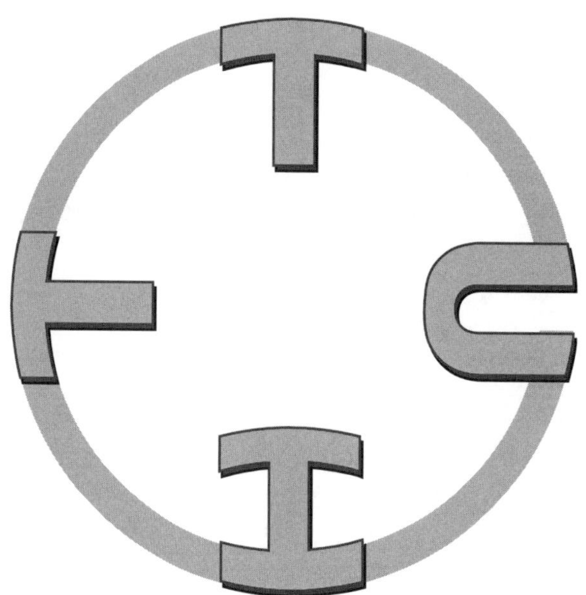

You just got a "ROUND TUIT"!

6. Do it now. Procrastination is a major time management obstacle. Putting things off creates a domino effect of problems. Wasted time, missed opportunities, poor performance, increased stress, and self-depreciation are just a few effects of procrastination. To avoid these issues:

   - Use the "Ben Franklin" method to offset negative excuses for procrastinating.

     On a sheet of paper, make two columns. Label one column "Excuse" and label the other column "Reality". Write the first excuse for not doing a task. "I am just not in the mood". Then respond to yourself in the "reality" column. "Mood will not do the work, but actions will. If I wait until I am in the mood I will never get this done. If I do not get this done, I will be penalized."

   - Use positive self-talk statements:

     - There is no time like the present.
     - The sooner I get this done, the sooner I can be with my friends.
     - I have easily done projects like this before.
     - I know I will feel better after getting this out of the way.

   - Break the larger goal into smaller pieces.

     Often, procrastination occurs when the objective seems overwhelming. Break the huge projects into tiny bits to be able to reach the big goal in a sequence of achievements. A whole of series of little goals will eventually make one big goal.

How do you eat an elephant?
The answer is one bite at a time.

TO DO LIST

A-1 Turn to term paper

B-1 Review notes with Maria

C-1 Return book to library

C-2 Call John about Friday

A-2 Review for math quiz

- Set priorities.
    - Write out a "To-Do" list.
    - After everything is listed, prioritize the list into "A, B, or C" priorities.
    - Then go back to the "A" category and prioritize that group 1, 2, 3, etc. Remember to break an overwhelming "A" into smaller chunks.
    - Set a time frame for each of the A-1, A-2, A-3 and so on.
    - Get started.

- Be organized.

  Have the materials, books and notes for the project readily available. Put all other material away that may be distracting. Eliminate clutter that might be "visual noise".

- Commit.

  Take the stance that you are going to do this. If others interrupt, tell them about your plans and goals. The person interrupting might also become a dedicated, study partner.

- Reward yourself.

  Congratulate yourself on a job well done. After the successful completion of the goal, plan to do something fun.

TRY THIS:

Before starting the next section on note taking, get a text book for any type of class.

Try out the ideas as you work through the information on "Studying Text Books"

STUDYING TEXT BOOKS

1. Get the global picture first.

- Read the title page and preface. Many students skip this step and jump in to the first chapter. The preface can give you clues as to how to study this particular text.

- Study the table of contents. Get a sense for the flow of the material. Look at it as though you were looking at a road map before taking a long trip in the car.

- Go to the back of the book and review the index. There may be key words that immediately grab your attention. Take some time to go to that section and read about that subject. This will not only get you motivated to go to other sections in the book, but it will also give you a feel for the author's writing style.

- Start in the first chapter and "skim" the book. Go through each chapter glancing at the topic headlines and subtopic key words. In a learning map format, jot down key words and page numbers of subject matter that seems really interesting.

- At the end of each chapter, read the summary all the way through. If there are questions to answer about the chapter, take the time to review the questions. Put a check mark by the ones you think you can answer already.

How could I have been more efficient studying for the last exam?

2. After getting the global picture, begin with the assigned chapter(s).

- Read one section of the chapter at a time.

- At the end of a section, imagine yourself as the teacher who is creating the test for this class. Write down one or more questions that you would ask if you were the teacher. Then answer the question.

- Repeat the same process with each section.

Note: *This process may seem more time consuming in the short term. In the long term, however, you will have saved yourself a significant amount of review time. More importantly, your long-term memory will be considerably stronger. You may also know the test questions in advance.*

3. Review the time and effort that was put in the first chapter you studied.

See if there is a way to be more efficient. Reset your time management schedule.

How did I personalize the information?

4. Personalize the information.

"Why do I need to know this information?" The answer could be as simple as "I need to pass this course and I need an "A".

"How is this going to help me in other classes?"

"Where are other places I could use this knowledge?"

"When am I going to apply this to my everyday life?"

"Whom can I talk to about this information?"

"What's in this for me?"

5. Engage Emotions

When reading difficult material that is mostly facts and figures, engage emotions by reading the material out loud. As you read, vary your accent. If the author is German, use a German accent. Put loud emphasis on some words and whisper others. Stand up as though you are giving a speech to five thousand people in an auditorium. Use gestures and animation as you read.

Remember, the brain likes the unusual and the outrageous.

Effective Note Taking

EFFECTIVE NOTE TAKING DURING LECTURES

You are familiar with taking notes during a lesson or lecture. However, simply writing what you are hearing does not ensure you are learning and remembering. There is a difference between passively taking notes and ACTIVELY being involved in making notes.

Note Taking is a Skill

Taking notes during a lecture is a skill that requires practice. Although there are some recommended note-taking techniques that will be explained, the objective is for you to personalize the principle to your own style.

Note Taking Can Be a Challenge

The spoken word is often more difficult to interpret than the written word. The lecturer may use words that are "relative" by nature. As mentioned earlier, your Analytical Mind defines words according to your base set of knowledge.

The spoken word disappears quickly. Unlike the written word, there is little or no time for analysis. This is especially true if the lecturer does not accept questions until the end, does not allow time for feedback, or is lecturing on some form of electronic medium.

Some lecturers are hard to follow because their speech lacks apparent organization. You may not be able to see the pattern or direction of the lecture until you are close to the end. That is when you wish you had taken different notes.

Notes provide a written record for review and analysis

Why Bother to Take Notes?

The most important reason is to help you remember what was said. While taking notes, the listener must condense or reframe the information. This process immediately relates the new information you already have.

Notes provide a written record for review and analysis. The notes can then be cross-referenced to your notes from related reading material and research.

When done properly, notes can make order out of chaos. Lectures can be disorganized or the speaker may be responding to random questions that are not linked. Notes can be re-written to tie all of the information together.

Before Taking Notes

If you have a choice, sit in a place where it is easy to see and hear. Avoid sitting next to doors to limit outside noise and visual distraction.

Make sure you have two pens, highlighters and colored markers. Ink is easier to read. Some notes may already be done if the speaker uses handouts or a syllabus. Highlighters save writing. Colored markers allow you to color code notes in the margins for organization and emphasis.

Label the notebook with the course name, date and topic. This will be important during the global course review at the end.

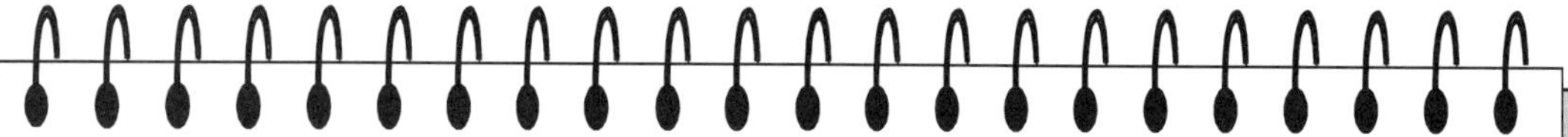

WHILE TAKING NOTES

- Main Ideas
- Record Details not in other sources
- Information written on the board could be test material
- Convert to your own words (Assimilate)

Prepare yourself mentally. Review your goal for the course. Compare your goal to the speaker's objectives. The two may be different and some blending of the two may be required.

Review your previous class notes, reading material, and, if appropriate, study group notes. Focus on adding to the material you have. Do not worry about the speaker's style. Some boring speakers may be providing a significant amount of information while the motivating speakers may just be providing excitement.

While Taking Notes

Getting every word is not important

Go for the main ideas only. Record details only as needed. Take notes on illustrations and how the information can be applied. It is not necessary to take notes on information you can find in another source.

Paraphrase what the speaker is saying

By converting what the speaker is saying into your own words, you are integrating the new information into information you already have (Assimilation). Be careful not to let your paradigms, preferences or prejudices get in the way of your focus on the subject.

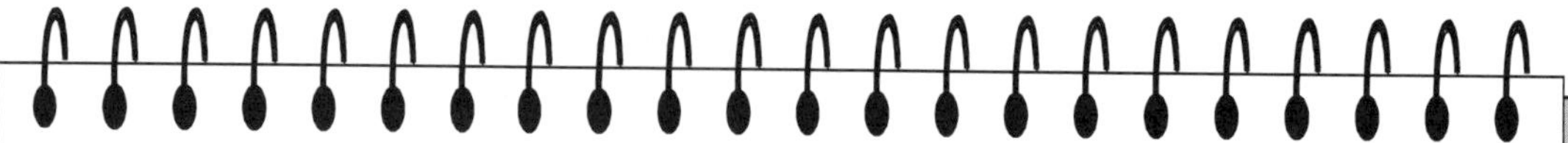

BE CONSISTENT

- Color code the same way
- Create your own symbols or "shorthand"
- Leave space to add supportive information
- Use "!" for real important information

Use a consistent system for emphasis and organization

Color-code your notes. One color could represent facts while another color may represent opinion. Highlighting and underlining in specific colors will help in the review process.

If you do not take shorthand or have not been trained to "speed write", then you need to develop your own system of abbreviations.

Leave plenty of "white space" on your notepad. You may want to come back to a point. Put a question mark by statements you do not fully understand. Once clarified, scratch out the question mark and write the qualifying statements in the white space.

Become an aggressive listener

If permitted or if possible, ask questions during the lecture. Discuss the implications of the information. Relate the information to current events or to other classes you are taking or have taken.

Be mentally ready. Go into the lecture with a positive attitude. Assume that you are going to leave the class with newly found knowledge that will help you in life, not just the class.

Make a conscious effort to stay focused on the speaker. The more you practice concentration skills, the easier it becomes. By reviewing your goals before the class, you will be listening for key information to fill gaps in your notes from previous lectures.

Stay flexible. Every speaker has a unique style. You must learn to stay consistent with your note-taking system and be able to adjust to the distinctive style of lecture.

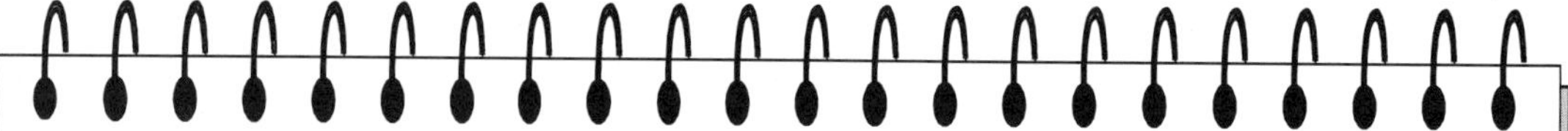

AFTER CLASS

- Review and reword
- Find answers to questions
- Write down additional questions
- Note ideas
- Review previous notes to link the classes together

After Taking Notes

Review and reword

As soon after the lecture as possible, rewrite your notes. Do not just recopy what you already have to make it more legible.

- Fill in blanks
- Add information from other sources
- Expand on ideas or concepts
- Finalize notes that are incomplete

Make reviews progressive

During scheduled study time (see study time management), add on previous notes with the most recent notes. The learning map technique is ideal for progressive note taking.

By using progressive reviews, you are rehearsing the earlier information. The major benefit is a significant saving of study time during midterms and finals. Cramming will be unnecessary!

Review notes in short segments

If a review of progressive information could take an hour to complete, break the review into four, fifteen-minute sessions. This gives the brain time to process and efficiently store the information for easy recall. The short review cycles also help reduce fatigue and increase the motivation to learn.

How do I currently review class notes?

What could I do better?

Review your notes with study partners' notes

When reviewing with one or more study partner, compare your notes to all others.

- This allows you to catch information you might have missed
- It creates discussion on emphasized information; i.e., you may have highlighted something that a partner found insignificant
- Comparing notes will help you get better at note taking techniques

Create mock test questions

Just like the reading techniques, you should project what exam questions could arise from the lecture or class discussion. If working in a study group, exchange questions with the other partners. Compare your answer to the others in the group.

Learning Map

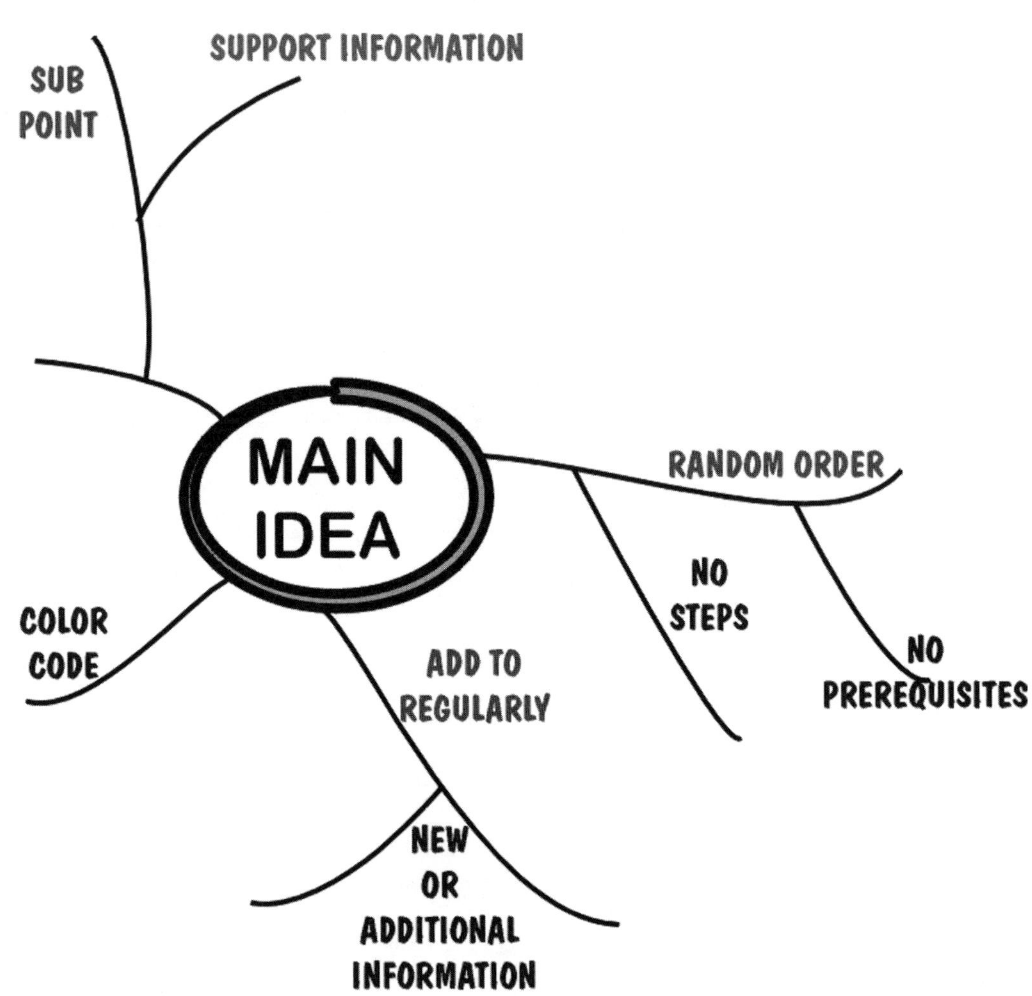

TECHNIQUES FOR TAKING NOTES

Learning Maps

(Review the information about learning maps from the "Introduction". You should have already practiced this technique.)

The main theme of the visual notes should be in the center of your page. Use a single word or picture if possible. As each new topic within the main theme is learned, a drawn representation should be added to the map. Link each new piece of information to the theme. Related information can branch from these pictures so that they become a visual "map" of what you are learning.

Why do learning maps work so well?

The brain doesn't work in a line-by-line way that notes are written. It randomly seeks previous information for association purposes. This is similar to the way learning maps are constructed: linking similar areas of learning together.

Using color helps when constructing learning maps because there is an added emotional link. Color also stimulates right brain thinking. And, as in the memory example, research suggests that a "picture can replace a thousand words".

Your Learning Maps dramatically increase your ability to learn your notes. You simply look at the Map you have created and then take a blank sheet and redraw the map. If there are blank areas in your new map due to lack of recall, spend more revision time on those areas.

Learning Maps are "Multi-Sensory"

Learning Maps use:

Kinesthetic	- Writing
Visual	- Seeing
Auditory External	- Listening
Auditory Internal	- Self-Talk

Taking Notes During Interactive Lectures

Interactive lectures encourage class participation and questions. The speaker is generally flexible and the material flows in reaction to the students' response.

Divide the note page into three sections.

Notes

Notes

The "Notes" section should take up approximately two-thirds of the page. The space leaves plenty of room for key words, ideas or diagrams. (See "Effective Note Taking During Lectures" page 99.)

Conclusions

Draw a line across the bottom of the page. About two inches from the bottom should be sufficient space.

As soon as possible after the end of the session, draw conclusions about the information on the page.

- Conclusions link the new information to your current base of knowledge
- Conclusions summarize key points
- Conclusions create relationships between previously unrelated concepts
- Conclusions can reinforce the global continuity
- Conclusions can strengthen meaningful, long-term memory

Anchors

Notes

Conclusions

Anchors

Draw a line from the top left of the page down to the "conclusion" line. Start about two inches in from the left of the page.

Anchors are memory tools that hold the information in place. Just like a boat anchor that prevents the boat from floating away, memory anchors help prevent the learning from floating away.

There are some anchors that you can make immediately through direct associations with your current understanding of the subject. Other, more difficult concepts may need additional thought.

Ideas on how to create an anchor should be noted in the box. The following memory anchor techniques are just a few ways anchors can be utilized.

- **Pictures & Posters**

  Make yourself posters of what you are learning. Have information displayed in your study area. Research from the University of Wisconsin has found that having lesson content on display visually can increase your retention by 40%.

- **Acronyms**

  N.A.S.A., NBC, CBS, ABC, and I.R.S. are all examples of acronyms in everyday use. F.I.R.E - U.P. is another. An acronym takes the first letter of each word in a series and forms another word from them. By recalling the acronym you recall the first letter of each word or step in a process, and the order in which the steps occur.

Charts

Brain Lobes

Parietal

- *Touch*

Frontal

- *Planning*
- *Decision-Making*

P

O

T

Occipital

- *Visual*

Temporal

- *Auditory*
- *Word Recognition*

Another type of acronym is shown by "Richard Of York Gave Battle In Vain" where the first letter of each word of the sentence is the first letter of the colors of the rainbow in the right order - Red, Orange, Yellow, Green, Blue, Indigo, and Violet.

Acronyms are especially useful if you want to remember the steps in a process in the correct order.

- **Flow Charts**

Flow Charts are graphic representations of a series of steps. Flow charts connect one phase of an activity to other phases. They can also show indirect relationships between the phases.

If studying Biology and the Digestive System, a flow chart could show what happens when a person ingests food. The flow chart will take different directions depending on the type of food and the body's nutritional requirements.

Flow charts are also excellent logic tools. The "if-then" technique can be applied. For example, "if I do step five and the result is X, then I go to step six. If I do step five and Y is the result, then I must back up to step four for corrective actions."

- **Organizational Charts**

Organizational Charts are designed to show a hierarchy or relationship tree. A corporation, for example, could have an organizational chart showing all employees and their reporting relationship. If studying Government, an organizational chart could show the President and the Cabinet members.

Organizational Charts can be used for showing groupings. If studying Biology, for example, the body parts could be grouped and categorized; i.e., the digestive system, the nervous system, etc.

What is the best way for me to learn dates?

What other techniques might work?

- Time-Line Charts

  Time-Line Charts show the time relationship between events. If studying history, a Time-Line Chart could describe the rise and fall of the Roman Empire.

Combining Charts

Often there is an overlap of the different charts. A Time-Line Chart may show the period when specific Roman Emperors reigned. An Organization Chart may be needed to show one particular Emperor's advisors. A Flow Chart may be needed to show that Emperor's accomplishments or failures.

WORK SMARTER, NOT HARDER

Although the information presented here may seem overwhelming, the fact is that it is quite simple when broken into pieces. You may already be doing many of these techniques but you were not consciously aware of the process.

Each of the tools will need to be adapted to your schedule, classes and current study habits. As you try the different techniques, adjust to the type of class. Vary the techniques within the same class to find the method of study that best suits you.

In order to become an outstanding learner, you have to get started.

Pick one class and FIRE-UP

Self Assessment

1. How well do I understand MY BRAIN?

2. How well do I understand MY MIND?

3. MEMORY: Have I identified at least 5 ways I can remember things better?

4. MOTIVATION: Have I completed the "investments and benefits" in the Hot-Air Balloon?

5. DAILY LEARNING JOURNAL: Am I keeping a record of my learning achievements?

6. Am I using the Learning Map?

7. POSTURE: Am I making use of the mind/body/brain connection to lift my confidence?

8. How do I react to fear and stress? Am I combating the "FIGHT OR FLIGHT" reaction with Conscious Mind control?

9. Am I using Affirmations to gain my positive sub-conscious?

10. Have I PLANNED my learning and review sessions to take account of what I now know about the best ways to learn - short sessions, frequent breaks and scheduled reviews?

SUMMARY - MODULE 1

In Module One there was a 3-4-5 approach to brain-based, accelerated learning.

The three divisions of the physical brain were discussed:

- Reptilian
- Mammalian
- Neo Cortex

We discovered four levels of the mind:

- Conscious
- Analytical
- Subconscious
- Instinctive

Within the brain and mind, there are five levels of memory:

- Short-Term Immediate
- Short-Term Working
- Short-Term Intermediate
- Long-Term Working
- Long-Term Archive

Within each of these foundational subjects, subtopics of Comfort Zone, Declarative Memory, Procedural Memory and memory techniques were described.

FOUNDATIONS

It Is Time To FIRE-UP

The Foundation module has now been covered. It is time to reflect on what you have learned so far. This is an "active program" therefore it is of little benefit to simply read the text. You need to get involved to learn better.

Throughout the introduction and this first module there have been exercises and activities for you to think about or complete. Each activity is adding to the learning process. Before moving on to the next module it is a good idea to evaluate what you know.

What are the top three concepts that I can apply immediately?

1 ____

____

2 ____

____

3 ____

____

CREATE A LEARNING MAP OF MODULE 1

What else do I need or want to know?

____

Where can I find the information?

____

Whom do I want to ask?

____

MODULE 2

Foundations

Intake Information

Real Meaning

Express Your Knowledge

Use Available Resources

Plan of Action

Learning Styles
INTAKE INFORMATION
Linear
Brick By Brick
Creative
Rhythm
Images
1600 Times Faster
Global
The Big Picture
Logical
Sequential
Language
Numbers
Analytical
Left Brain
Right Brain
ORGANIZATION

MODULE 2

I - INTAKE INFORMATION

Overview 129
In and Out of Style 131
Learning Style Intake 133
Your Sensory Preference 133
Learning Styles and Sensory Preferences 141
Three Key Learning Styles 143
Visual 145
Auditory 151
Kinesthetic 157
Multi Sensory Intake 163
Organizational Preferences 165
Global Learner 167
Linear Learner 169
Get the "Organized, Big Picture" 171
Hemispheric Preference 173
Summary - Module 2 181

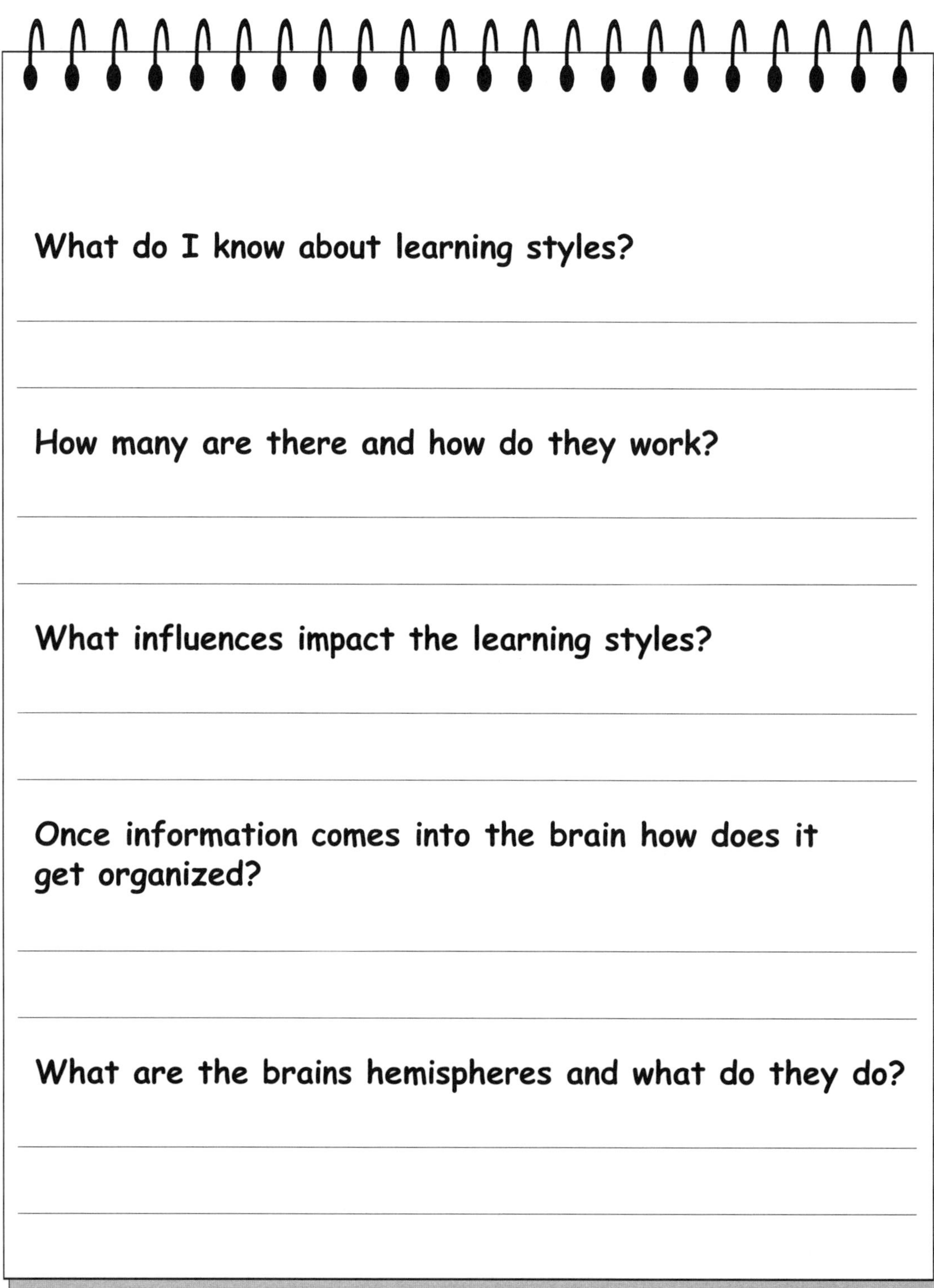
What do I know about learning styles?
How many are there and how do they work?
What influences impact the learning styles?
Once information comes into the brain how does it get organized?
What are the brains hemispheres and what do they do?

I - INTAKE INFORMATION

Overview

It has been estimated that the average human being uses between five and ten percent of the brain's capacity. If we were able to tap into just 50%, there would be no language barriers because we would all be able to speak any language. There would be no need for computers to solve math problems or scientific equations because the brain works faster than any computer. Books could be read in minutes instead of hours.

THIS MODULE CONCENTRATES ON THE WAY YOU TAKE IN THE INFORMATION

One of the ways to begin to unlock the tremendous potential that you have locked away in your brain is to discover the way you bring information into your brain. This intake of information is accomplished through your own personal learning style.

UNDERSTAND YOUR LEARNING STYLE

This module concentrates on the way you take in the information. First is to look at the various ways we get information. Then there will be personal explorations to discover the preferences that make up your individual learning style.

TRY THIS:

1. Fold your arms. Note which arm lies on top.
2. Now change so the other arm is on top.

How did that feel?

IN AND OUT OF STYLE

Once you understand your individual style, techniques will be explored that will enhance that learning style and make your learning more efficient and enjoyable.

In school, there may be a mismatch between the teaching style and your learning style. If a mismatch occurs, it is useful to know how to convert the teacher's style into a learning style compatible with your own. The knowledge gained in this module will also help you make that conversion into a style that works for you.

EACH PERSON HAS A NATURAL, COMFORTABLE WAY OF LEARNING

When asked to perform a function that is not "natural" such as crossing your arms a different way, an awkward hesitation generally occurs. You must think hard about the change. When you first folded your arms it was easy, natural, and you just did it without thinking. When asked to change, it became more difficult and you needed to concentrate.

This is a simple demonstration of doing something "In-Style", the natural way you do it, and doing something "Out of Style".

Learning is similar. Each person has a natural, comfortable way of learning. When forced to learn in a way not compatible with this style, frustration sets in. When learning is difficult, especially when caused by an incompatible style, self-blame is generally the result.

Everyone has the same potential as the students who excel at learning. All you need to do is find the learning style that is uniquely appropriate to maximizing your learning efficiency. Once found, you can become a competent, confident learner.

Learning Style Intake

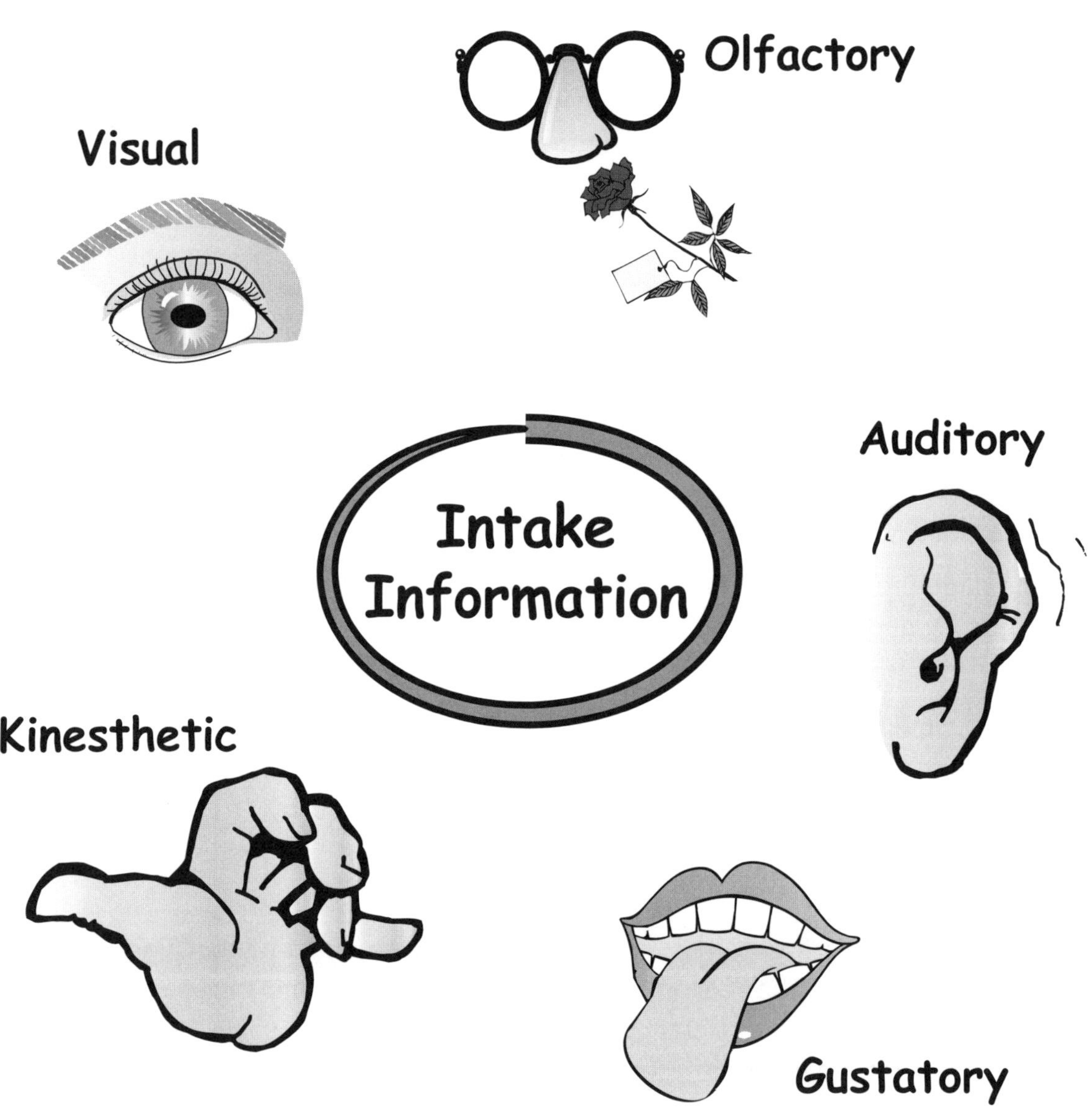

LEARNING STYLE - INTAKE

The first part of your individual learning style is made up of the ways you take in information or data. This involves the areas of:

- Sensory Preference
- Organizational Preference
- Hemispheric Preference

Your Sensory Preference

Intake starts with your senses. Everything you sense, you store in one of the layers of memory. As far as science knows, the only way for information to enter the brain is through the five senses.

When presented with new information we either:

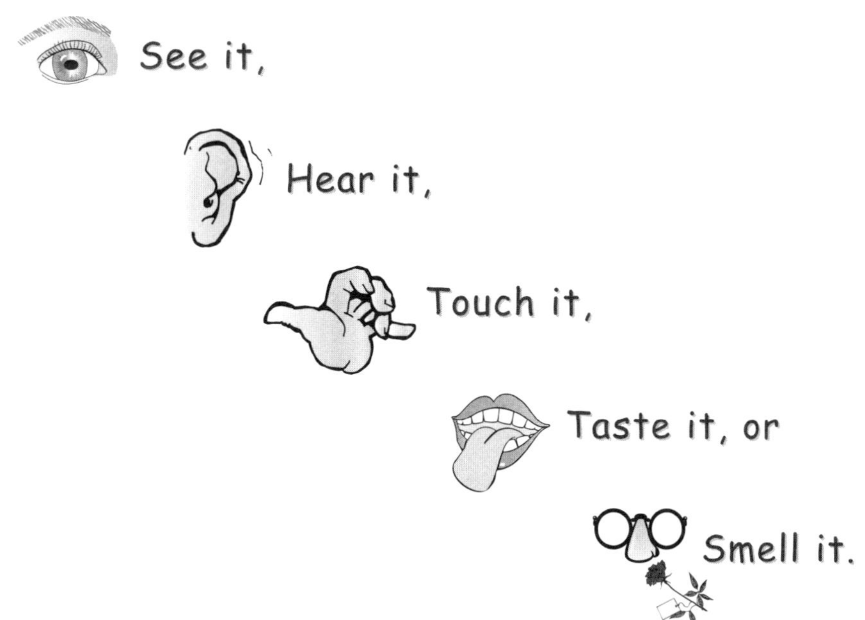

ASSESSING YOUR SENSORY PREFERENCES

As opposed to a test, the following is an indication of how you deal with obtaining information. Select the one answer for each statement that most represents the way you react in that situation:

1. **When you talk do you:**

   - ❑ Speak quite fast?
   - ❑ Speak at a medium pace?
   - ❑ Speak slowly?

2. **Do you best remember:**

   - ❑ Events, happenings, emotions?
   - ❑ People, surroundings, faces?
   - ❑ What is said, sounds, names?

3. **Do you memorize by:**

   - ❑ Repeating the words possibly aloud?
   - ❑ Writing repeatedly?
   - ❑ Walking around, doing repeatedly?

4. **Are you distracted by:**

- ☐ Movement?
- ☐ Things around you?
- ☐ Sounds?

5. **When you spell a word do you:**

- ☐ Visualize the word?
- ☐ Write it down?
- ☐ Sound it out aloud?

6. **Do you prefer:**

- ☐ Music?
- ☐ Paintings?
- ☐ Dance/sport?

7. **When following assembly instructions do you:**

- ☐ Like to work with the pieces?
- ☐ Follow diagrams best?
- ☐ Like to be told how to?

8. **Are you more likely to say:**

- ☐ Looks good?
- ☐ Feels good?
- ☐ Sounds good?

9. **When reading do you:**

- ☐ Move your lips when reading to yourself?
- ☐ Prefer to read to yourself?
- ☐ Run your finger along the line?

10. **Recalling the beach what comes to mind first:**

- ☐ The feel of the sand or feeling of peace?
- ☐ The sight of the ocean and beach?
- ☐ The sound of the waves and the breeze?

11. **When going to sleep what's most important:**

- ☐ A darkened room?
- ☐ A quiet room?
- ☐ A comfortable bed?

RESULTS

Check your responses with the following and at the end total up how many "V", "A" and "K" responses you selected.

1. When you talk do you:

V Speak quite fast?

A Speak at a medium pace?

K Speak slowly?

2. Do you remember best:

K Events, happenings, emotions?

V People, surroundings, faces?

A What is said, sounds, names?

3. Do you memorize by:

A Repeating the words possibly aloud?

V Writing repeatedly?

K Walking around, doing repeatedly?

4. Are you distracted by:

K Movement?

V Things around you?

A Sounds?

5. **When you spell a word do you:**

   V Visualize the word?

   K Write it down?

   A Sound it out aloud?

6. **Do you prefer:**

   A Music?

   V Paintings?

   K Dance/sport?

7. **When following assembly instructions do you:**

   K Like to work with the pieces?

   V Follow diagrams best?

   A Like to be told how to?

8. **Are you more likely to say:**

   V Looks good?

   K Feels good?

   A Sounds good?

9. **When reading do you:**

   A Move your lips when reading to yourself?

   V Prefer to read to yourself?

   K Run your finger along the line?

10. **Recalling the beach what comes to mind first:**

   K The feel of the sand or feeling of peace?

   V The sight of the ocean and beach?

   A The sound of the waves and the breeze?

11. **When going to sleep what's most important:**

   V A darkened room?

   A A quiet room?

   K A comfortable bed?

(V) VISUAL ____________

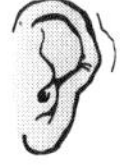

(A) AUDITORY ____________

(K) KINESTHETIC ____________

For an extended, electronic learning style test, log on to: www.fire-up.com

Learning about chocolate

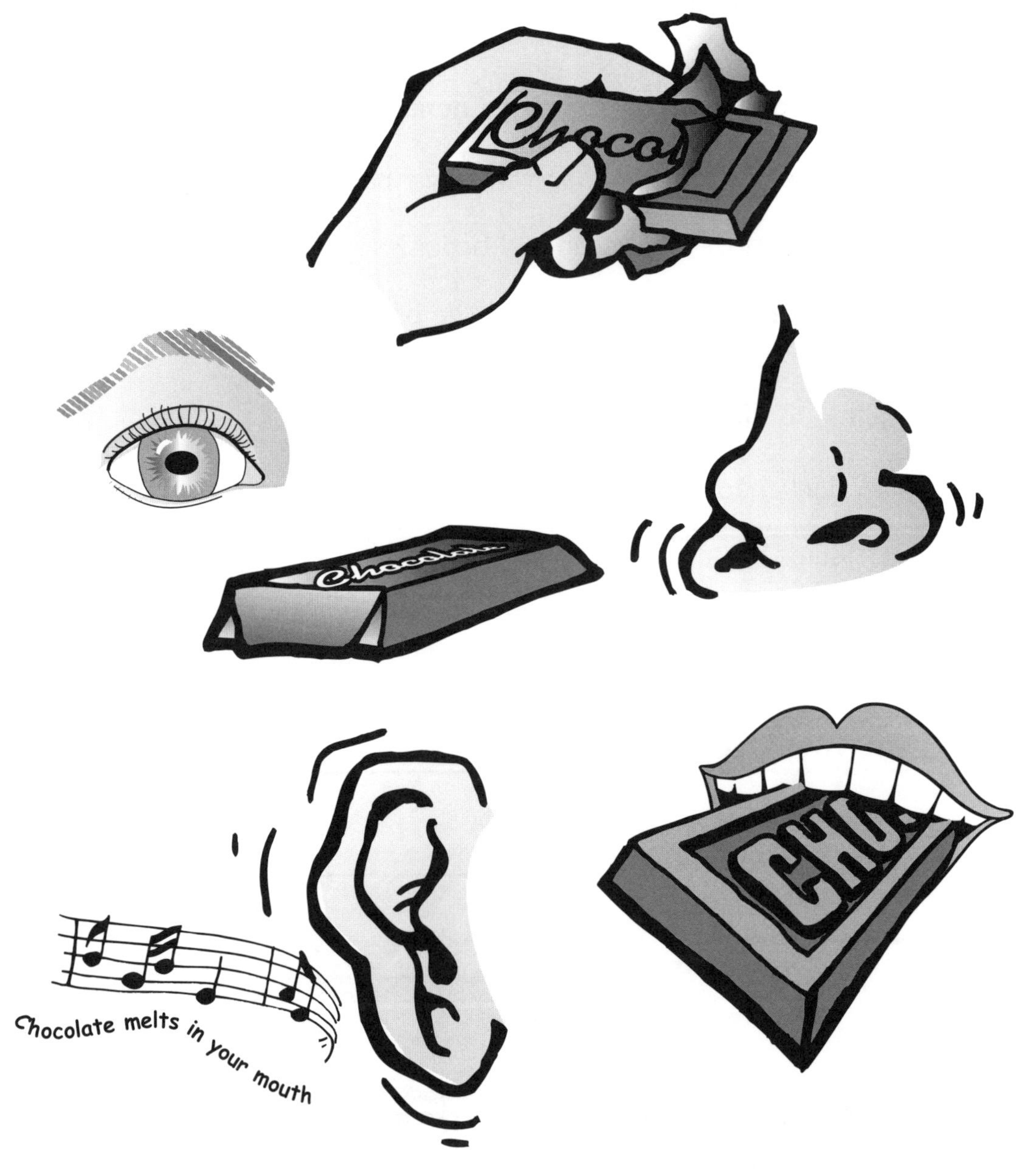

LEARNING STYLES AND SENSORY PREFERENCES

There are techniques that are naturally used to gain information. The most natural channel of intake represents your preferred Learning Style. It is possible, however, to learn to use techniques that are not necessarily associated with your primary channel.

THE MOST NATURAL CHANNEL OF INTAKE REPRESENTS THE PREFERRED LEARNING STYLE

Everyone is Unique! Some people learn primarily by using auditory skills to process information that is heard. Others primarily use visual skills to process the same information. Visuals like to see a picture or information in writing. Still others like to use physical or experiential skills. A primarily Physical Learner, also called a Kinesthetic Learner, likes to touch the equipment and learns well through role-plays.

AUDITORY SKILLS

You also learn everytime you taste or smell something. No one uses the five senses in isolation, but the senses are used in a combination unique to each individual and the learning situation.

VISUAL SKILLS

The more ways a person can take in information, the more the information is reinforced and the absorption of the data is enhanced.

PHYSICAL OR EXPERIENTIAL SKILLS

When studying a subject that you find difficult or that you are having difficulty remembering, try learning the information using a different style.

Combining the sense with the stimuli influence

There are six Sensory Preferences:

Visual	-	External
Visual	-	Internal
Auditory	-	External
Auditory	-	Internal
Kinesthetic	-	External
Kinesthetic	-	Internal

Any stimulus impacting the five senses facilitates Learner Intake. There are five traditional Learner Intake Styles:

- **AUDITORY** (hear)
- **KINESTHETIC** (feel/touch)
- **VISUAL** (see)
- **OLFACTORY** (smell)
- **GUSTATORY** (taste)

Stimuli can be generated from two key sources:

- **INTERNAL**
- **EXTERNAL**

THREE KEY LEARNING STYLES

We will focus on the three main Learning Styles of Visual, Auditory and Kinesthetic. Olfactory Learning Style (sense of smell) and the Gustatory Learning Style (sense of taste) will have limited application. Both, however, are powerful learning processes. Use these when studying a cooking class, chemistry, or other classes where these two senses would be appropriate.

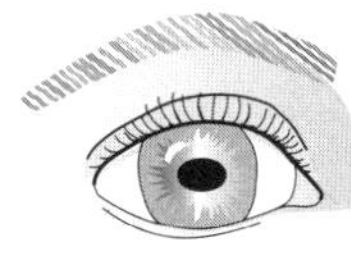

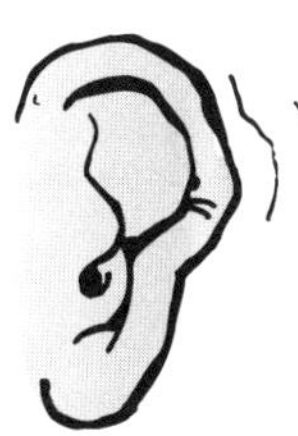

Visual External

What will work for me? ______________

VISUAL - EXTERNAL

The Visual-External learner processes information through seeing. Visuals like to follow the pictures and read the directions. The Visual-External learners would prefer art to music. They speak quickly, but their responses are generally short and in monotone. The Visual-External learners tend to doodle while listening. They learn by writing research papers. They memorize through visual associations.

Visual-External learners accept things for how those things look. They, for example, may buy a shirt based on how it looks versus how it feels. Visual-External learners must be colorful and visually organized. Learning Maps, bright post-it notes and highlighted notes are valuable tools.

The Visual-External learners can learn in a flexible environment. Noise is not a distraction. The exception to their flexibility is someone sitting in their space or blocking their view. Visual-External learners need to sit where everything is in view.

The Visual-External learners will use phrases like, "Do you **see** what I am saying?" They also prefer to want to "see" what a speaker is saying. If a speaker is in one room and the learner in another, the visual will go to the room where the speaker is.

TO DO

Sketch, plan or draw a diagram of something you are learning.

Learning as a Visual-External Learner

For the visual person, seeing information is vital. Visuals typically reach for pen and paper to explain something or to remember something. They would rather draw you a map than tell you directions.

Sketching

Make a sketch, plan, flow chart or diagram of what you are learning. This visual representation may make it more meaningful for you. If a subject is presented using plenty of graphics, posters, charts and diagrams, a visual person will find it easier to absorb the facts.

Highlighting

When reading a text, use a highlighter pen to identify NEW information. Using color will engage the emotional centers of the brain and the emotions assist in building strong memories.

Visual Internal

What will work for me? ______________

VISUAL - INTERNAL

The **Visual-Internal learners** can readily **envision** a concept. Often the Visual Internal learners will close their eyes and create a picture of the subject matter in their mind. The picture will be detailed and concrete.

Visual Internal learners tend to add, subtract or modify the pictures as new information impacts the scenario. The new vision can easily be described in minute details.

Learning as a Visual-Internal Learner

Imagine and Learn

Close your eyes and use your imagination to paint a mental picture of what you are learning. "A picture is worth a thousand words" applies to mental pictures too.

If your subject is history, for example, imagine you are there seeing the people and watching the action. In your imagination, become one of the characters of the time and mentally act out the episode you are learning about.

Whatever your topic, becoming a mental artist can be a powerful way to be or do what would otherwise be impossible. Only in your mind can you travel around inside the human body or inside a computer processor.

Auditory External

What will work for me? _______________

AUDITORY - EXTERNAL

Auditory-External learners gain knowledge through hearing. Interpersonal skills are extremely important since Auditory Learners like to have someone "talk them through it". They prefer listening to a tape instead of reading a book. The Auditory Learner will remember what is said over what was seen.

The Auditory-External learners will tend to be interdependent. The learner will want to work in a group or in pairs. The Auditory-External can work alone, but they enjoy helping others in a group. Successful acquisition of a subject matter is directly correlated to the success of the group.

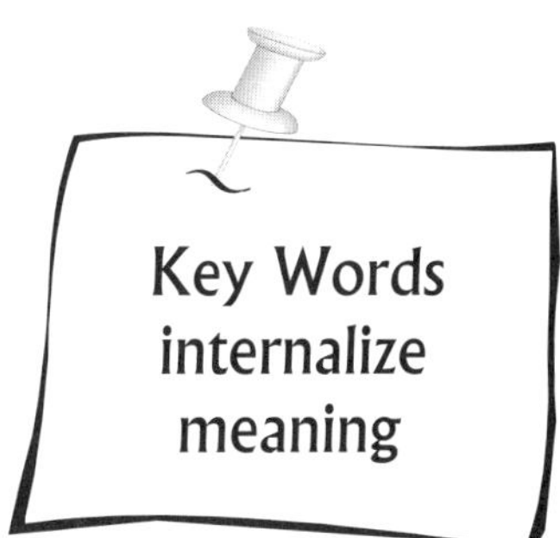

The Auditory-External learners will telegraph their learning style by using phrases like "Do you **hear** what I am saying?" or "**Listen** up people".

Learning as an Auditory Learner

Learning as an Auditory-External Learner

Auditory people love the spoken word. Auditory Learners enjoy either hearing the information or delivering the information. They enjoy discussing with others what they are learning and have no problems extracting the data they need from listening to lectures or audio tapes on the subject.

Read Aloud

It helps auditory learners to hear what they are reading. Reading aloud so you can hear your own voice is a technique that helps this learning style. The tones used can be varied to make what is being read more memorable.

Remember that the brain likes things that are odd or unusual. You can try reading sections using a foreign accent or even reading in a whisper to keep your brain interested.

Use Audio Tapes

Record lectures, or classes so that you can replay them again later. Record what you are reading. If listening to information is a technique that works for you, make use of "downtime" such as while driving, listen to your tapes.

Learn With A Friend

Auditory people like to both talk and discuss, therefore learning with a friend that you can discuss the subject with is a great way to utilize your auditory strengths.

Auditory - Internal

What will work for me? ___________

AUDITORY - INTERNAL

The Auditory-Internal learners use Intrapersonal Intelligence (discussed in Module 4) because they often question, debate and talk to themselves. "What is this subject going to mean to me?" "I already know a lot of this stuff." "How am I ever going to learn this?"

The Auditory-Internal learners tend to be independent. They prefer to work alone. Others have a tendency to interrupt their internal conversations. The Auditory-Internal learners can work in small groups or pairs, but become less effective in a noisy, talkative environment.

Learning as an Auditory-Internal Learner

Build in some quiet time for reflection on a subject. Before a group exercise, take a few moments to think through the project before beginning discussions. This will allow for focus on what is already known about the subject as well as what is not known.

At the end of a class discussion, jot down key words relating to what was learned. These main topic words will stimulate an internal discussion on what happened during the class.

Kinesthetic-External

What will work for me? _______________

KINESTHETIC-EXTERNAL

Kinesthetic-External learners are sometimes called Tactile or Physical Learners. They absorb information through moving, doing and touching. Kinesthetic Learners will think best as they are pacing. They have a tendency to gesture frequently or have exaggerated facial expressions during conversations. Kinesthetic Learners can remember subjects or locations best when they have actually experienced the subject.

The Kinesthetic-External learners tend to be field-dependent. They prefer to learn in the contextual environment. Field trips, hands-on experiments, and real life applications are most important. Kinesthetic-External learners want to try it first then read about what they just did. Textbooks and lectures are of little value. On the other hand, action novels are motivating.

Kinesthetic-External learners often use "concrete-action" or "feeling" words. "Are you **following** me?" "We need to **lock** this project down." "This idea **feels** good."

Learning as a Kinesthetic-External Learner

Provide yourself with an action environment. Charades, miming or picture drawing games can generate strong learner intake.

A Kinesthetic person needs to get physically involved in what they are learning. Hands-on activities: making a model, walking through a process, or physically acting out a scenario are all things that help the Kinesthetic person to get the data they need. A Kinesthetic will rather demonstrate something than draw it out or verbally describe it.

Kinesthetic Learners like to be emotionally involved

Get Involved With Your Reading

Have a pen or pencil and physically underline NEW important information. Highlighting, as a Visual Learner does, is also a useful technique for the Kinesthetic. This is especially true if you use colors that appeal to the emotional centers of the brain. (Remember Kinesthetic Learners also like to be emotionally involved.)

Check It Off

When reading, make a check mark at the end of each paragraph as you complete and understand it. This lets you physically tell your brain you have understood that section. Use To-Do lists and check off the items as you complete the tasks. This gives the kinesthetics a sense of physically demonstrating they are progressing and moving forward.

Walk Around

A kinesthetic person finds it hard to sit still! If possible walk around while you are reading or listening.

Make Maps

While making a map of your notes might seem like a visual pursuit, the physical action of writing or drawing is a kinesthetic activity. When making map notes you are physically involved and therefore you are using your kinesthetic sense of touch.

Act It Out

Make up a role-play and physically act out what you are learning. If studying classical music, while listening you could conduct the orchestra performing Bach's Brandenburg Concerto No. 5.

Kinesthetic - Internal

What will work for me? _______________

KINESTHETIC - INTERNAL

Kinesthetic-Internal learners prefer a learning environment that allows them to make inferences about the subject. They are sensitive to most all non-verbal signals such as tone, inflection, tempo, gestures and facial expressions. Emphasis on inferences and non-verbal signals means that **how** a person says something is more important than **what** is said.

Kinesthetic-Internal learners need to have a positive feeling toward a subject matter. Any uneasy feelings lead toward learning blocks or information storage interference. They need to understand and positively accept the "What's In It For Me" (from the radio station WII-FM).

Kinesthetic-Internal learners will be less verbally expressive. They prefer not to raise their hand in class because they are internalizing questions and answers. When asking how Kinesthetic-Internal learners are dealing with a subject, their response might be "I am **feeling** my way through this".

- Paint mental pictures
- Create metaphors
- Watch video-taped demonstrations
- Observe role-play
- Watch Movies Related to your subject

Learning as a Kinesthetic-Internal Learner

Answer the question, "Why do I need to know this?" This can be done in a variety of ways depending on the class. In a math class, for example, develop the top five ways that this algebraic formula can be used in the next ninety days.

Multi-Sensory Intake

What will work for me? ____________________

MULTI-SENSORY INTAKE

The more ways you can explore your subject, the more information you will obtain. You should get into the habit of not just relying on the one main sensory channel you prefer, but adding other elements to create multi-sensory learning.

Learning Maps are an ideal, multi-sensory intake method. This is especially true when the teacher is in the lecture mode. Learning Maps will help convert the presentation style (auditory) into your preferred style if it is different. When creating learning maps you:

HEAR the information,

PHYSICALLY draw the map

VISUALLY see what you are drawing

The more ways you can explore your subject, the more information you will obtain.

Post-It Notes

These brightly colored reminders can be used either to make notes of key points or locate them in a textbook. This tool is great for studying when you cannot write in the book (Library or text book). Physically move the notes around and relate them to each other.

Flash Cards

Using 3 x 5 cards, record new information in short notes, key words or definitions. Flash Cards can be kept in a pocket or purse to act as a quick review of learning.

Brick
by
Brick
Linear

The Big Picture
Global

ORGANIZATIONAL PREFERENCES

Global or Linear Organizational Preference

Although Auditory, Visual and Kinesthetic learning styles are the most common, there are influences that act as processors or information organizers to enhance a particular style. These processors are directly associated with the learning styles.

Each person has a preference for how information is stored in the mind and in the brain. In the mind, you may want to store information in an orderly fashion as a Linear Learner. Or, you may prefer to see the big picture first as a Global Learner. Understanding the Organizational Preferences is an important step in preparing to learn.

Global Learners need to see the "big picture" first. Global Learners want to fit pieces together on their own. If the Global Learners do not understand the overall direction of the program, they are not interested until the program is over.

Global Learners need to understand the relevance or purpose of the information. For information organization, relevance goes beyond the WIIFM described for Kinesthetic-Internal learners. The purpose for Global Learners is more thematic by nature. If the lesson starts with 1 and ends with 10, what thread connects lessons 2 through 9 to 1 and 10? The answer is sometimes as simple as a story line to a lesson or a case study with a complex theme.

Learning as a Global Learner

Learning as a Global Learner

- Global Learners like to multi-task.
- They can work on theory and practical application at the same time.
- Sometimes appearing to be disorganized, Global Learners jump from problem to problem or manage two or three problems at the same time. Often to a Global Learner "close enough is good enough". If a problem is 90% solved, the last 10% can be inferred.
- Most often, Global Learners are right-brain thinkers. They process pictures, symbolic events and themes.
- Instead of targeting a subject with bullet point precision, the Global Learners tend to use a shotgun approach. Shoot a wide pattern at the subject and then focus on what hit the target.
- Global Learners are not discouraged by ideas that missed the target because there are a significant number of creative ideas that are close to the bulls-eye.

GLOBAL LEARNERS NEED TO SEE THE "BIG PICTURE" FIRST

GLOBAL LEARNERS LIKE TO MULTI-TASK

GLOBAL LEARNERS PROCESS PICTURES, SYMBOLIC EVENTS AND THEMES

Get an overview of the program, the day, and the lesson. Use of metaphors, case histories and practical application benefit the big picture learner best.

Keep in mind that Global Learners need to see the entire picture to organize their mind to accept information. They constantly need to look at the picture on a jigsaw puzzle box (global outcome) in order to complete the assembly. Learning Maps are a significant aid.

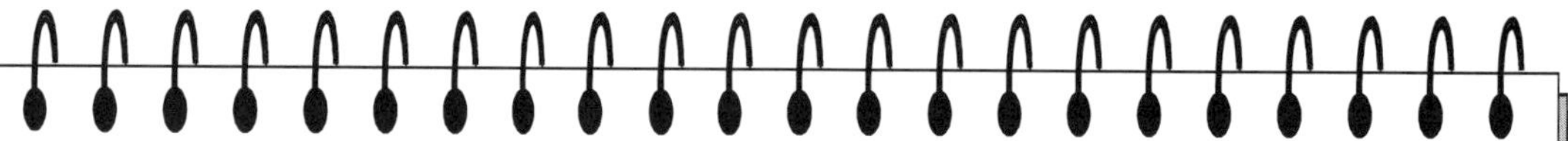

Which do you think you are?

☐ I like to know the whole story up-front.

(GLOBAL)

☐ I like to work step-by-step in a logical progression.

(LINEAR)

You may check both boxes. The key is the one that you checked first. Instead of putting a check mark in the box, write weighted numbers that will add up to 100. You may be for example, 70 Global and 30 Linear

Learning as a Linear Learner

Linear Learners, on the other hand, want a very specific flow of information. "Follow the book" is the Linear Learner's slogan. Linear learners take one step at a time, complete the step, and then ask, "What's next?" The Linear learner stays focused on a single task. They can work on multiple tasks at the same time if the tasks are sequenced.

TO DO

IDENTIFY WHAT YOU ALREADY KNOW ABOUT THE SUBJECT

Linear Learners are analytical by nature. They will compare and contrast facts or sets of information. Qualifying type questions are generally asked the most.

Linear Learners are usually word-based learners. Words must be defined in concrete terms in order to be able to compare different sets of information. Presenters are often held specifically to their words.

Because of the desire for structure, Linear Learners maximize their left-brain capabilities. This usually makes them good at math, language, computers or any sequential type task.

TO DO

FOCUS YOUR BRAIN ON AREAS WHERE YOU NEED NEW INFORMATION

Although they appear to have a global desire to understand the long-term plan, organizationally that information is for planning or preparing for the next step.

Key points must have a full and detailed set of information. Justification for a subject must be built up through a logical progression. Written materials are important and the traditional outline format must be present.

Time needs to be taken for an objective analysis of the subject. Although the Linear Learner enjoys creativity, they truly dislike surprises; i.e., pop quizzes, spot role-plays, etc.

The "Organized" Big Picture

GET THE "ORGANIZED, BIG PICTURE"

Whether you identify yourself as a Global or Linear Learner, you can benefit from over-viewing the subject you are learning and gaining a "Big Picture". You can achieve this by reading the chapter headings and scanning the Table of Content.

TO DO

IF YOU HAVE AN INSTRUCTOR, ASK FOR A VERBAL OVERVIEW OF THE WHOLE CLASS OR COURSE

If you have an instructor, ask the teacher to give you a verbal overview of the whole class or course. Make a learning map as the teacher gives you that overview. This will ensure you have an idea of where your learning will take you and where the pieces all fit in.

The map is like having the picture on the front of a jigsaw box. It helps you to organize your learning in a linear format and gets your brain ready to accommodate new information in specified areas.

Gaining an overview at the beginning of a learning session will also help you identify what you already know about the subject. It is rare that a person will begin a subject with a zero base of knowledge. Examine what you already know before you begin.

The overview can focus your brain on areas where you need new information and areas where you have basic knowledge that requires expanding.

Hemispheric Preferences

The left side of the brain is the logical, sequential and analytical side of the brain

The right brain is the side that uses imagery, rhythms and emotions to accept and store information

Logical

Sequential

Language

Numbers

Analytical

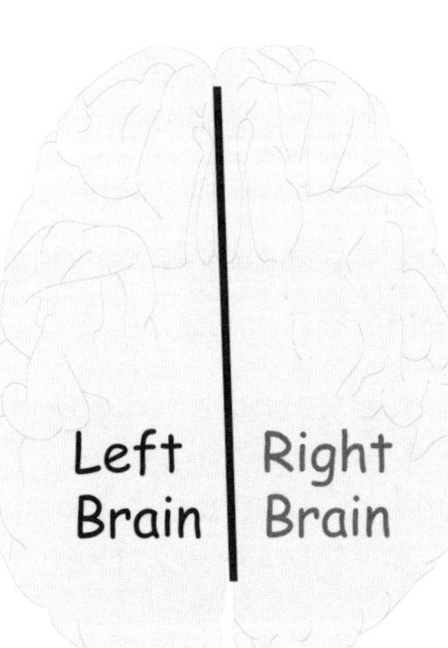

1600 Times Faster

HEMISPHERIC PREFERENCE

The brain is divided into two halves called hemispheres. The Left Hemisphere and the Right Hemisphere each manage specific functions. Although there are some technical difficulties with the Right-Left Brain Theory, the general concepts can help explain another learning preference.

LEFT HEMISPHERE

RIGHT HEMISPHERE

Some people have a tendency to use their left-brain more than their right. The left side of the brain is the logical, sequential and analytical side of the brain.

Others have a tendency to utilize the right side of the brain more than the left. The right brain is the side that uses imagery, rhythms and emotions to accept and store information. Through the use of music, case studies, colors, role-plays and other Accelerated Learning methods, the right hemisphere can be actively involved in the learning process.

Both hemispheres work together. It is false to assume that a person is a "right-brain individual". In Accelerated Learning you will actively use both "sides" of the brain.

BOTH HEMISPHERES WORK TOGETHER

Often "left-brained" people are wrongly thought to be uncreative. The logic, sequence and analysis in the left-brain can, in reality, generate exceedingly creative thoughts. Albert Einstein would be a prime example.

On the other hand, artists who appear to be strict "right-brain people" must use logic and rules about shapes, colors, and combinations in order to produce the work of art.

Create a poem or rhyme for a subject you are studying.

Recent studies on the right-left brain technology have shown that the left-brain has a tendency to process information in parts. The left-brain works sequentially through lists in order to draw some conclusion.

The right brain works differently. It scans randomly all the parts at once making the right side between 400 and 1600 times faster than the left side.

THE LEFT-BRAIN HAS A TENDENCY TO PROCESS INFORMATION IN PARTS

By actively using both sides of the brain at once you can increase the effectiveness of your learning. Think how easy it is to remember the words of a popular song. The learning did not consciously take place. The words just seemed to be remembered with no real effort.

Words are a function of the left-brain while music is generally dealt with by the right brain. Put the two together and you have much more efficient learning with less conscious effort.

THE RIGHT-BRAIN SCANS RANDOMLY

Rhyming works just as well as having music. For example, to remember which months have 30 days and which have 31 days, many use:

**"Thirty days has September,
April, June and November".**

This is a combination of words (left brain) and rhyme (right-brain). This powerful tool is used only too well in advertising jingles!

21 Answer Technique for Creativity
1
2
3
4
5
6
7
8
9
10
11
12
13
14
15
16
17
18
19
20
21

Allow Time For Creativity

Learning is accomplished in a left-brained environment. In order to truly learn, however, right-brained creativity is also needed. Because of the traditional, logical, step-by-step approach to most learning, people tend to access the left-brain first when thinking about the contextual information.

In the exercise below you will see that the left-brain must reach its capacity before the creativity of the right brain can be activated. In other words, don't give up too soon. Always allow time for the right brain to kick in to give you new suggestions.

Try This:

How many uses can you think of for a pencil? In the box on the opposite page write as many as you can. Be as creative as possible. Write one use along side each number until you can reach the target of 21 ideas. Do not stop until you have really exhausted the possibilities. Do not think about or analyze your ideas; simply continue until you have reached 21.

Select a subject you have been assigned.
Describe 21 ways you can use this information?
1
2
3
4
5
6
7
8
9
10
11
12
13
14
15
16
17
18
19
20
21

What Happens:

Typically you will find you paused after the first seven ideas (plus or minus 2) and again after 14. The theory behind this is that the mind has a tendency to work in groups of 3s and 7s (chunking).

The first seven tend to be "left-brain" answers because you were posed with a left-brain question. Once the left-brain is out of ideas, the right brain becomes involved and you begin to accelerate your creativity. There is a balance between left and right for the next seven. The last seven tend to be "right brain" answers.

This is a great technique for brainstorming in a group. It forces you to get into the creative ideas formed by the right brain after you have "emptied" the more logical left brain of ideas. The key is not to give up too early and not to analyze the ideas until you have finished.

Self Assessment

As in Module One, there are ten areas to review and assess just how well you have understood and are implementing these techniques.

1. I understand the difference between a Global Learner and a Linear Learner and I have identified myself as mainly a ________ learner.

2. I do/do not (strike out one) need a Big Picture Overview and I understand the reasons for having one.

3. I have identified my Assimilation style(s) and incorporated them in my learning preparation.

4. I understand the general differences in the way the two sides of the brain deal with information and identify myself as primarily ______ -brained.

5. I have completed my Sensory Assessment and have found I use _______ as my primary intake style.

6. I have practiced visual ways of learning.

7. I have practiced auditory ways of learning.

8. I have practiced kinesthetic ways of learning.

9. I have practiced multi-sensory ways of learning.

10. When communicating I try to take into account the style of my listeners as indicated by the words they use.

SUMMARY - MODULE 2

In Module One, the Foundations of Accelerated Learning techniques were described. The brain, the mind and the levels of memory were introduced. In Module Two, the foundational information was expanded to describe how information is brought into the brain and mind.

Anything that impacts the five senses causes learning to take place. Learning is taken in through:

- Visual Intake - the need to see something to learn it
- Auditory Intake - the need to hear something to learn it
- Kinesthetic Intake - the need to touch or experience something to learn it
- Olfactory Intake - the need to smell something to learn it
- Gustatory Intake - the need to taste something to learn it

The three used most often are Visual, Auditory and Kinesthetic. With these three, there are two influences that impact the intake process: Internal Influences and External Influences.

If learning a subject using the preferred learning style does not work, switching to another style for more efficient intake is the best approach. Review techniques for each style (pages 145 - 161).

Information that comes into the brain gets organized. Mentally, the mind is concerned with making the information part of a global picture or specifically lining up the information in a linear fashion.

The brain physically puts information in either the right hemisphere or the left hemisphere. Both sides constantly communicate with each other.

CREATE A LEARNING MAP OF MODULE 2

What else do I need or want to know?

____

Where can I find the information?

____

Whom can I ask?

____

MODULE 3

Foundations

Intake Information

Real Meaning

Express Your Knowledge

Use Available Resources

Plan of Action

Contrary
Association
Apples To Oranges
Apples To Apples
Scientific
Impetuous
REAL MEANING
New Knowledge
Current Knowledge
Independent
Social

MODULE 3

F - FOUNDATIONS

R - Real Meaning 187

Assimilation Preference 189

Assimilation Preferences Profile 191

Association Assimilators 193

Contrary Assimilators 193

Impetuous Assimilators 195

Scientific Assimilators 195

Social Assimilators 197

Independent Assimilators 197

Summary - Module 3 199

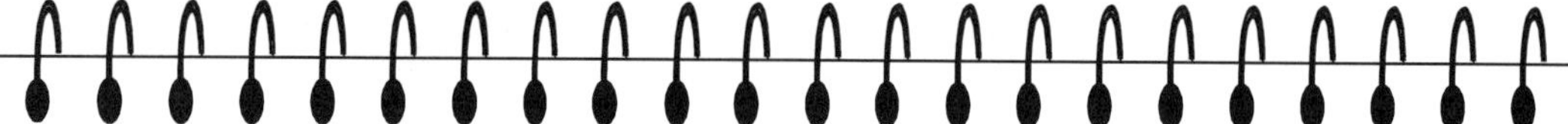

Assimilation

How do I connect new information to knowledge I already have?

Do I compare similarities?

Do I contrast or challenge information?

Do I jump in?

Do I break a project into pieces and then reassemble those pieces?

Do I need to talk to others about what I have learned?

Do I prefer to work alone first and then talk later?

Do I change Assimilation Styles according to what I am trying to learn?

R - REAL MEANING

Overview

So far the Foundational mechanics of the brain and mind have been described. The Foundation was expanded to include Information Intake with the different Learning Styles.

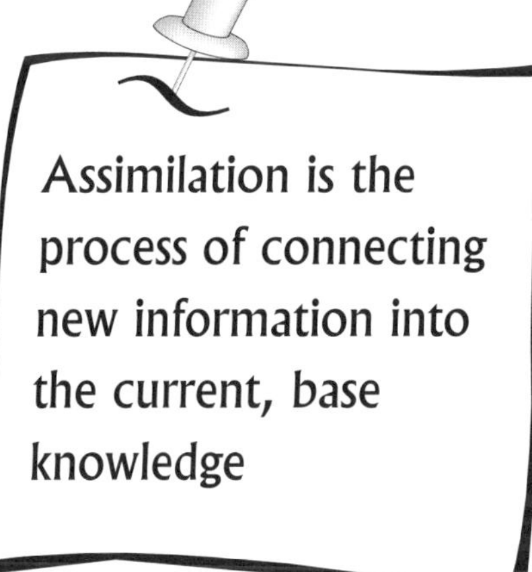

In order to store the information in a long-term working memory and in a place that is easily accessible, Real Meaning must be given to that information. Real Meaning is created when you are able to "Assimilate" or blend the new information with knowledge that is already meaningful to you.

The next issue is what to do with the information we have just brought in during the Intake process. As was learned in Module 1, meaningless information is usually "Archived". Rote memory, Declarative memory, and at times, numbers are basically meaningless.

Assimilation - adding new information into current, base knowledge

ASSIMILATION PREFERENCE

Assimilation is the process of connecting new information into the current, base knowledge.

When one or more of the learning styles is impacted by new information, the brain Accommodates or makes room for the previously unknown material. This sets up the process of Assimilation or the process of connecting Accommodated information to previously known information.

If you already have some base knowledge of the information, then Assimilation of new information will start taking place immediately. If, on the other hand, you have had no previous experience with the new information, the learner must create a connection.

For example, when an English speaker is learning Spanish as a second language, the English speaker will immediately create associations with words with common context. "Hola" is Hello.

On the other hand, if that same English speaker was attempting to learn a language where the written word looks like a "doodle" and the pronunciation has no resemblance to any word in English, Assimilation is difficult at best.

Constantly Ask

What do I know about this subject?

____

____

What do I need to know?

____

____

What would I like to know?

____

____

ASSIMILATION PREFERENCES PROFILE

There are six Assimilation Preferences that can be used in learning new information. All six are used based on the learning environment. Rank the following preferences from 1 (your strongest preference) to 6 (barely or never use). They are:

Association _____I associate new learning to things I already know. I use analogies and stories to help me understand.

Contrary _____I challenge and question what I am learning; new learning has to stand on its own.

Impulsive _____I just jump in and get on with learning without thinking about it or planning it.

Systematic _____I logically organize the data so it makes sense. It must be orderly and step-by-step.

Social _____I like to talk about the information with others. I find they help me to get the information I need.

Independent _____I like to work on the information independently. I need my own space to learn.

Assimilators

ASSOCIATION ASSIMILATORS

CONTRARY ASSIMILATORS

Association Assimilators

The Association Assimilators are constantly comparing information for similarities. Association Assimilators look for consistencies and how information fits together. They tend to be more agreeable and are mostly habit-driven.

ASSOCIATION ASSIMILATORS LOOK FOR CONSISTENCIES AND HOW INFORMATION FITS TOGETHER

Association Assimilators will want to see how an application has been done in the past and then how that application fits today's plan. Unassociated games or exercises are often irritating to the Association Assimilators.

Contrary Assimilators

The Contrary Assimilators process by determining what is wrong, different, missing or inconsistent. They will find flaws in logical progressions or discussions.

CONTRARY ASSIMILATORS ASSIMILATE BY ARGUING, TESTING, AND EXPLORING VARIATIONS

On the surface, Contrary Assimilators appear to be negative. "Yes, but", "What if", and other general challenges are the rule and not the exception. The appearance of negativity, however, is not necessarily a negative attitude. Instead, these learners assimilate by arguing, testing, and exploring variations. Traditional lesson plans and blatant predictability are strongly resisted.

Assimilators

Impetuous Assimilators

"Ready, shoot, aim" is the motto of the Impetuous Assimilators. Grab it, play with it, experiment, and if all else fails, read the directions. Impetuous Assimilators work in the "here and now" since they are so focused on figuring out the current problem. They at times will seem obsessed with a particular project. Once solved, however, the Assimilation is solid and long lasting.

IMPETUOUS ASSIMILATORS WORK IN THE "HERE AND NOW" SINCE THEY ARE SO FOCUSED ON FIGURING OUT THE CURRENT PROBLEM

Scientific Assimilators

The Scientific Assimilators are analytical and pragmatic. They respond by watching and absorbing information. Scientific Assimilators often stand back and watch an Impulsive Assimilator go through a series of trials and errors. Then they suddenly move in and change one or two elements that solve the problem.

SCIENTIFIC ASSIMILATORS ARE ANALYTICAL AND PRAGMATIC

Scientific Assimilators process by reflecting on potential or future events. The Linear Learning style tends to be prevalent.

Assimilators

SOCIAL
ASSIMILATORS

INDEPENDENT
ASSIMILATORS

Social Assimilators

The Social Assimilators are openly concerned about what others think, say or do. Their learning is influenced by peers, panels, or socially accepted subject matter experts. Assimilation takes place by comparing the new information to external societal norms.

SOCIAL ASSIMILATORS ARE INFLUENCED BY PEERS, PANELS, OR SOCIALLY ACCEPTED SUBJECT MATTER EXPERTS

Social Assimilators like to see behavior demonstrated and will take part in a role-play AFTER observing several models and critiques. The Social Assimilators will tend to ask; "Can you show me one more time how you want me to do this?"

Independent Assimilators

The Independent Assimilators make up their own minds about specific information. They assimilate by comparing and contrasting internally. Independent Assimilators are willing to accept information from others, but resist letting others influence their opinion about that information. "I will judge that for myself." They do not openly challenge other's opinions, but instead just ignore those opinions.

INDEPENDENT ASSIMILATORS ARE WILLING TO ACCEPT INFORMATION FROM OTHERS, BUT RESIST LETTING OTHERS INFLUENCE THEIR OPINION ABOUT THAT INFORMATION

SELF ASSESSMENT

As in the other modules, there are ten areas to review and assess just how well you have understood and are implementing these techniques.

1. I understand the general concept of Assimilation.
2. I understand how the Association Assimilator works.
3. I understand how the Contrary Assimilator works.
4. I understand how the Impetuous Assimilator works.
5. I understand how the Scientific Assimilator works.
6. I understand how the Social Assimilator works.
7. I understand how the Independent Assimilator works.
8. I know that the real meaning comes from the way I assimilate the information. I also know that real meaning is important in order to store information in the Working Memory. Therefore, I know that if I am not assimilating information with my main preference, I need to try a different approach.
9. I have practiced the different Assimilation preferences.
10. I have made a Learning Map of this module. (Page 200)

SUMMARY - MODULE 3

Every learner has all six Assimilation styles. Just like Learner Intake and Information Processing Styles, the Assimilation styles are prioritized for each learner. Even though every learner will be consistent, each learner has the ability to cross the line to a different style based on the current set of circumstances.

This means that the learner can develop a variety of strategies to blend new information into the current set that exists. If you are naturally an Association Assimilator but are having difficulty with a particular subject, then try a Contrary approach or a Scientific approach to the same subject.

The good news is that you are not locked into any one assimilation style. You can change assimilation style with subject matter. You can change assimilation style depending on the Teacher.

CREATE A LEARNING MAP OF MODULE 3

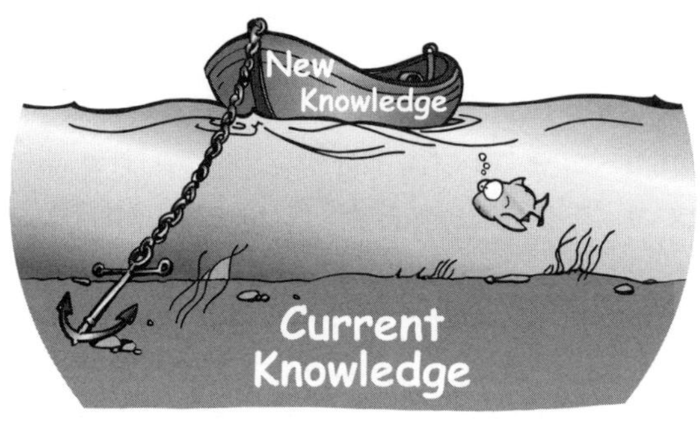

What else do I need or want to know?

____

Where can I find the information?

____

Whom can I ask?

____

MODULE 4

Foundations

Intake Information

Real Meaning

Express Your Knowledge

Use Available Resources

Plan of Action

INTERPERSONAL
LINGUISTIC
LOGICAL
EXPRESS YOUR KNOWLEDGE
INTRAPERSONAL
MUSICAL
KINESTHETIC
NATURALIST
SPATIAL

MODULE 4

E - EXPRESS YOUR KNOWLEDGE

Overview 205
An Intelligent Person 209
Multiple Task Learning 213
Using Logical Intelligence 213
Using Your Linguistic Intelligence 217
Using your Interpersonal Intelligence 219
Using your Intra-Personal Intelligence 223
Using Your Musical Intelligence 225
Using Your Naturalist Intelligence 229
Using Your Spatial Intelligence 231
Using your Kinesthetic Intelligence 233
Show You Know Through Practice 239
Testing Yourself 239
- Learning Maps 243
- Flashcards 245
- Imagination 247
- Learning Together 247
- Teach or Tell 249
- Role Play 251

Stepping Stones 255
Summary - Module 4 257

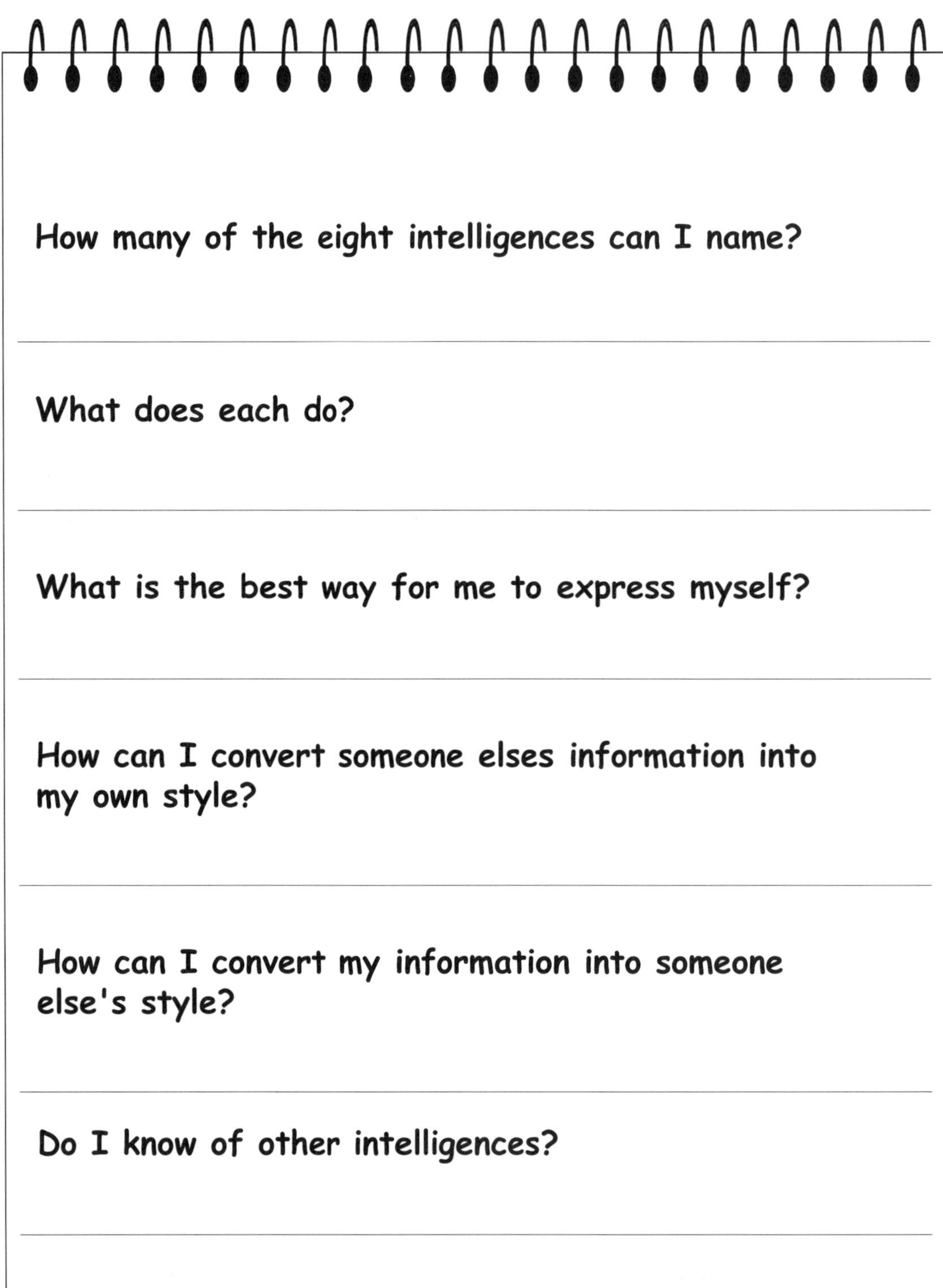

How many of the eight intelligences can I name?
What does each do?
What is the best way for me to express myself?
How can I convert someone elses information into my own style?
How can I convert my information into someone else's style?
Do I know of other intelligences?

E - EXPRESS YOUR KNOWLEDGE

OVERVIEW

You now have the basic ingredients to understand your learning style:

FOUNDATIONS - You know the building blocks. You were born with an amazing brain, mind and memory. You appreciate the huge capacity you possess to learn lifelong. You know you can train your memory. In essence, you can be what you want to be!

INTAKE - You have identified your unique preferences for taking in information through your senses and reviewed different techniques to enhance and expand your natural style.

REAL MEANING - You understand that you need to explore information in different ways before it becomes fully understood. Assimilation of information takes place once the real meaning of the information is discovered.

What's Left?

Letting others know you know.

The Learning Process

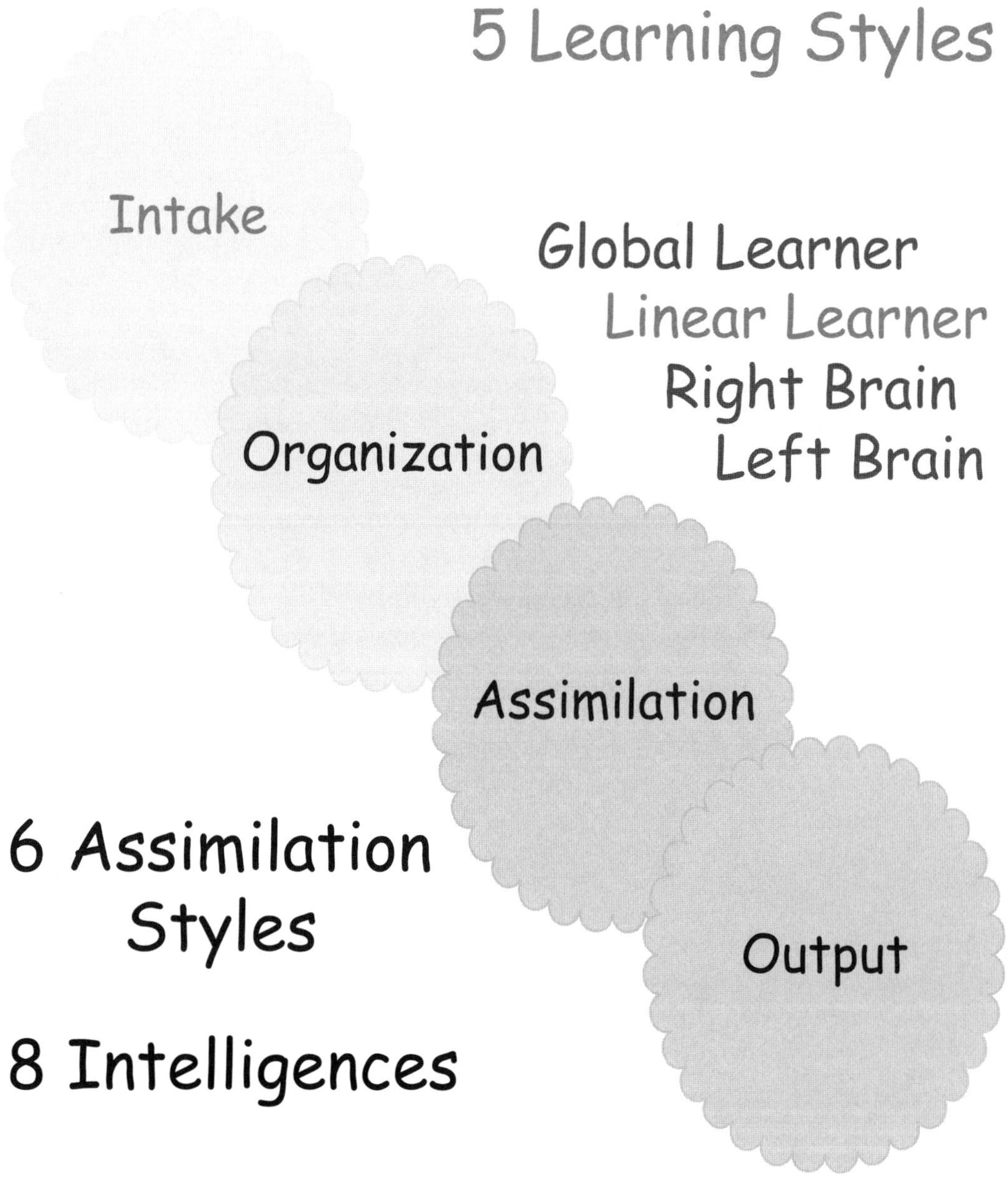

5 Learning Styles

Intake

Global Learner
Linear Learner
Right Brain
Left Brain

Organization

Assimilation

6 Assimilation Styles

Output

8 Intelligences

When you tell others what you know, you are also telling yourself what you really know and what you do not know. When you discover what you do not know or cannot remember, revisit the subject, intake the information differently, and use a new technique to assimilate the real meaning.

When you tell others what you know, you are also telling yourself what you really know and what you do not know.

The other key point in expressing knowledge to others is that showing you know overlaps the assimilation process. The learning process does not take place in isolated buckets of information.

LEARNING IS A MULTI-TASK PROCESS

Intake is overlapped by Organization.

Organization is overlapped by Assimilation.

Assimilation is overlapped by Intelligence.

In this Module, methods are explored that allow you to Express the knowledge gained and evaluate the quality of the learning.

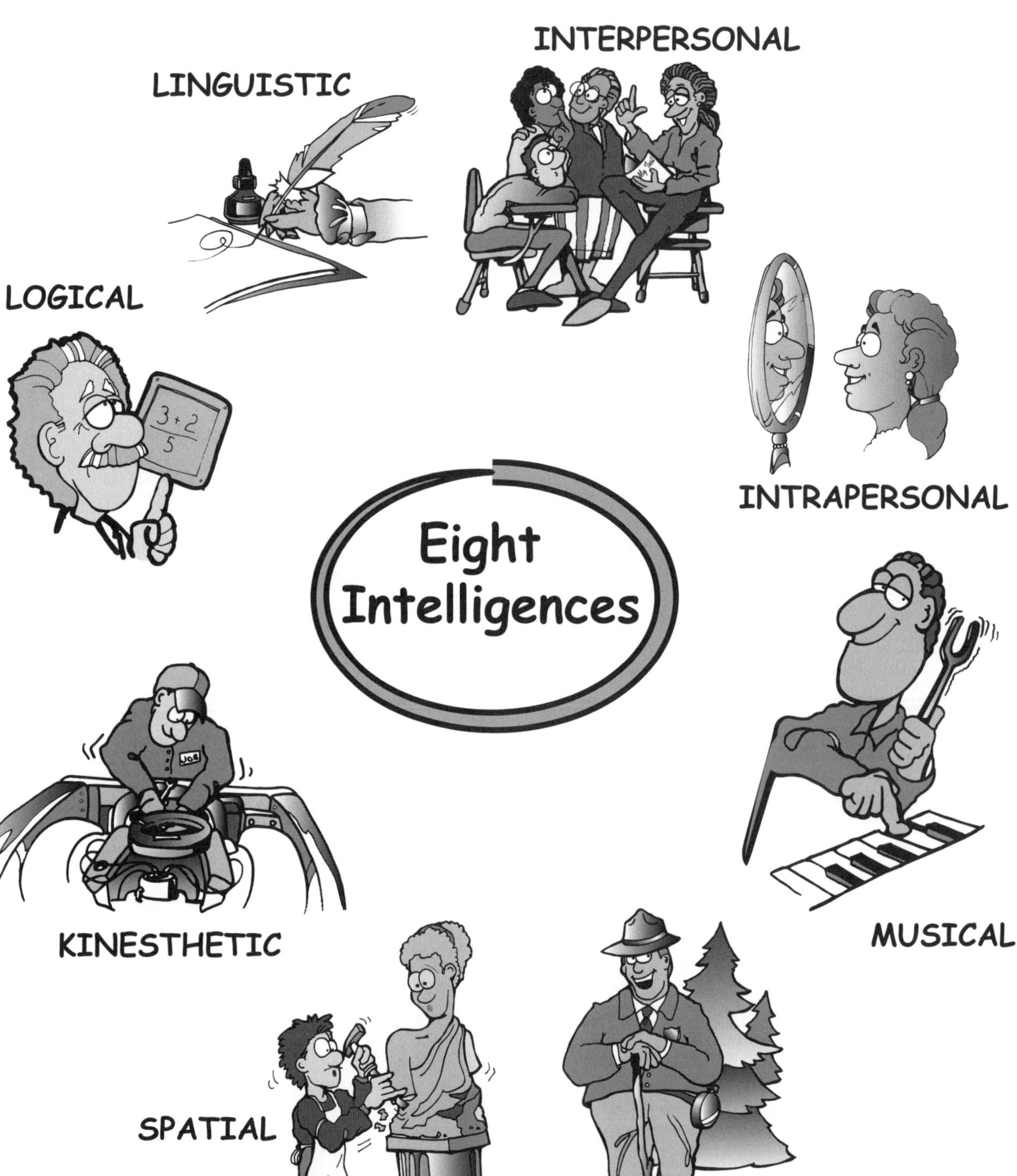
INTERPERSONAL
LINGUISTIC
LOGICAL
3+2
5
INTRAPERSONAL
Eight
Intelligences
JOE
MUSICAL
KINESTHETIC
SPATIAL
NATURALIST

AN INTELLIGENT PERSON

By definition, an intelligent person is one who has the capacity to comprehend information, reason the facts and communicate the knowledge.

Howard Gardner, a noted specialist in intelligence studies, proposes that there are eight distinct intelligences that are inherent in each of us.

In your mind, take a trip to the country of LLIIMNSK where all of the most intelligent people in the world live. They use every one of the eight intelligences to capacity.

L - Logical

L - Linguistic

I - Interpersonal

I - Intrapersonal

M - Musical

N - Naturalistic

S - Spatial

K - Kinesthetic

This module uses the extensive research by Dr. Howard Gardner. To expand your knowledge, please reference his book *Frames of Mind: The Theory of Multiple Intelligences* (1983, 1993) Published by BasicBooks.

Everyone has all intelligences.

Each person prioritizes the intelligences to create personal preferences.

Intelligence changes as the learning environment changes.

LOGICAL - Mathematical is another name for this intelligence that uses sequential analysis to come to specific conclusions. Scientists, accountants or economists focus on this intelligence.

LINGUISTIC - This is a skill of words. Writers or professional speakers emphasize this intelligence.

INTERPERSONAL - An ability to communicate well and to observe non-verbal signals is the foundation of this intelligence. Although linguistic intelligence is sometimes used, it is a teacher or a counselor that best utilizes interpersonal intelligence.

INTRAPERSONAL - Self-reflection characterizes the person who uses this intelligence the most. The ability to define and redirect goals based on past performance is key. Strategic planners or researchers have an inclination toward this intelligence.

MUSICAL - Creating and categorizing complex sounds is a characteristic of people who prefer this intelligence. A musician or sound editor may be examples.

NATURALIST - The Naturalist Intelligence is the ability to observe, understand and organize patterns or elements in a natural environment. The intelligence could belong to anyone from a Molecular Biologist to a Forensics Scientist.

SPATIAL - Visual abilities are an important element to this intelligence. A sculptor, for example, can "see" a block of stone as a beautiful work. Architects and Engineers stress this part of their intelligence the most.

KINESTHETIC - Physical intelligence is exemplified by people who are "good with their hands" or who are "natural athletes". Surgeons, Mechanics and Professional Dancers are inclined to function best with this intelligence.

Logical Intelligence

MULTIPLE TASK LEARNING

Learners need and often prefer other ways to explore a subject.

If only one method of learning is available, the student will be severely limited and may very well struggle with certain material.

Using multiple intakes, organizational preferences, assimilations and intelligences gives the learner a significantly greater network of connections. Information is stored more efficiently in various parts of the brain. The result is easier recall and procedural knowledge application.

USING LOGICAL INTELLIGENCE

Number or Rate Key Concepts

Rating the important points of a subject forces you to think carefully about what you are learning. It is difficult to rank the points without comparing them. It is also difficult to compare points without considering the real meaning of each point.

Analyze What You Are Learning

Do not accept all information at face value. When you use a system to be analytical, you are maximizing your logical intelligence!

WHAT WILL WORK FOR ME?______________________________

____

Create an A.E.I.O.U. learning map.

Add information important to you.

FOLLOW THE A.E.I.O.U. SYSTEM.

A - What ASSUMPTIONS are being made?

Is this the only point of view? Has anything been left out? Has the author used exceptions to make a general sweeping conclusion?

E - What is the EVIDENCE for this?

Does the information deal with facts or opinion? If it is opinion, is the person giving the opinion credible? If it is fact, what backup exists? What other explanations can there be?

I - Can I think of a good ILLUSTRATION or example of this?

What current knowledge can be associated with this information? Based on my own experience, does this information make sense?

O - What OPINION or conclusions can I draw about this?

Does anyone else have this opinion? Are the opinions justified?

U - What are the UNIQUE points in this?

What is different? What stands out?

Linguistic Intelligence

USING YOUR LINGUISTIC INTELLIGENCE

Re-Word Information

It is difficult to learn words written by somebody else. When you put what you have heard or read into your own words, you are required to understand it.

Brainstorm from memory all the things you feel you have learned. Write them down or say them into a tape recorder.

Skim through the pages of the study material to add further thoughts. Be careful to put these into your own words.

When you are reading, stop at the end of each main section and mentally review the key ideas in your own words.

Take notes in your own words and note the questions that arise from what you've learned.

Interpersonal Intelligence

USING YOUR INTERPERSONAL INTELLIGENCE

Teach what you've learned

The best way to learn is to teach. "Teach-backs" are a way of finding out what you know and what you do not know. The teaching concept will also dramatically enhance your procedural knowledge of the subject because your "student" will ask you to apply what you just explained.

Teaching requires you to collect your thoughts in logical order and put the ideas in your own words.

An additional benefit comes in the form of cross training. When you share information with others, they may have information you need to fill some information gaps. The addendum may or may not be in the text being studied. It is bonus information.

Compare Notes

The simple act of comparing notes with a friend at the end of a class or book is another way that cross training takes place. The study partners will understand or remember things you didn't, and vice versa. The simple reason for this is Intake, Organization and Assimilation preferences that are different from yours.

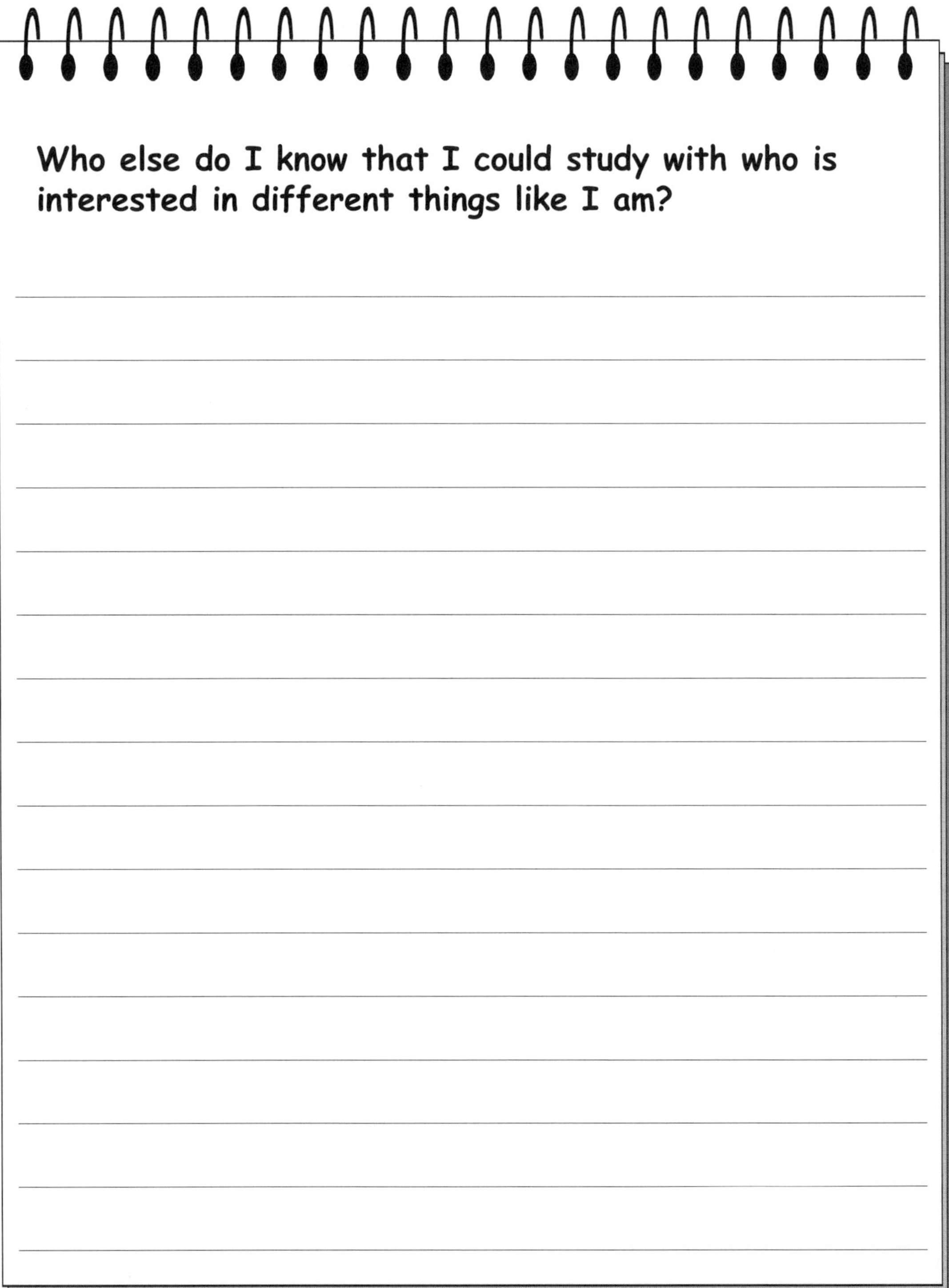
Who else do I know that I could study with who is interested in different things like I am?

LEARNING ACTION CIRCLES

Pick a group of students whose area of focus is different from one another. You could have a group with people whose major area of study includes math, science, history, teaching, and management. Five to seven people will be more than enough.

Select a consistent time to meet each week. Select a topic for that week. Discuss the topic from different perspectives. Allow opinions to flow during the discussions. Resist the urge to use the Fight-Flight instinct when someone challenges your belief system.

Not only will you learn new ways to look at information, you will learn to listen and investigate. Once you draw a conclusion after the research, the information will be more efficiently assimilated into you memory network.

Intra-Personal Intelligence

USING YOUR INTRA-PERSONAL INTELLIGENCE

Look for Personal Significance

If you are interested in a subject, you are motivated to learn. Researchers tested students' memory for paintings. Some just looked at the paintings while others were given information about the painting and the painter. The latter group remembered the paintings twice as well.

Once you've discovered the personal significance, genuine interest follows. People, the unusual, and unexpected connections make subjects interesting.

Investigate the Background Information

If the subject is art, what was in the creator's mind? What did the artist do differently from anyone else before? What new technique evolved?

Take Time for Reflection

Take time to reflect on the subject. Does the information fit in with what you know already? What are the benefits for you in the future?

The more real or 'concrete' you make the new information, the greater the chance of efficient assimilation.

Music should be instrumental only

ACTIVE
CONCERT

PASSIVE
CONCERT

USING YOUR MUSICAL INTELLIGENCE

Write a Song, Jingle, Poem or Rap

Advertisers take advantage of this technique to implant information in the listeners. Some of the most memorable advertising messages are presented in jingles or slogans that rhyme. Years later you still remember the commercial.

TO DO

> TRY TO CITE THE ALPHABET WITHOUT THE RHYTHM THAT WAS USED WHEN YOU LEARNED IT. OR, JUST GO FROM "A" TO "F" LEAVING OUT THE LETTER "C".
>
> DID YOU PAUSE AT "C"? YES/NO?

Try to cite the alphabet without the rhythm that was used when you learned. Or, just go from "A" to "F" leaving out the letter "C". Did you pause at "C"?

A rhythmic pattern makes the words highly memorable because you are activating both hemispheres of the brain, linking information with a continuous flow. When the beginning of the flow is activated, the rest of the flow falls into place.

The type of music is important!

Research shows that there is a direct relationship between music and the physiology of the body. Music can alter your mood and it can help your learning by invoking positive emotions.

Background music

Music stimulates the emotional center of the brain and the corresponding memories that are strongly linked to the sounds. Playing background music as you learn has proven to be a powerful tool.

For your private study you can use music in two different ways: an Active Concert and a Passive Concert. The music should be **instrumental only**. Words with the music will detract from what you are learning. Vary the tempo of the music you use based on the subject matter. Heavy metal type music restricts learning by altering the brain's chemistry. Studies have shown that students scored lower on academic tests after listening to heavy metal music.

The Active Concert

If it is an activity you are conducting, then use an energizing, upbeat tempo, with several instruments playing at the same time. This will stimulate the whole brain. Active Concerts are used for creativity and information output.

The Passive Concert

Use music of about 60 beats a minute and similar instruments (all string instruments) to relax you before you start learning, or when you are reviewing your work. The Passive Concert is used when "intaking" information.

If you find the music is disruptive during study, turn it off or turn it down. The music is designed to stimulate. If it interferes, adjust or eliminate. TV and Radio is highly disruptive and interferes with the intake process.

The Naturalist Intelligence

Nature Reservations

Blending Natural Ingredients

Classifications of Objects

Farming and Gardening

USING YOUR NATURALIST INTELLIGENCE

In 1996, Howard Gardner, the one who defined the seven intelligences, added the Naturalist Intelligence as the eighth.

The Naturalist Intelligence is the ability to observe, understand and organize patterns or elements in a natural environment. A Naturalist, for example, is one who shows expertise in the recognition and classification of plants, animals and insects. The intelligence could be found in a molecular biologist or, in some cultures, a "medicine man".

George Washington, Carver, Darwin, and Galileo are some who may qualify for the Naturalist Intelligence. Others may include a child who sorts and collects baseball cards; a chef who can sort and interchange ingredients; or, a Forensic Scientist.

Strategies to develop the Naturalist Intelligence could include:

- Collecting data on natural events (weather, volcanoes, etc.)
- Nature hikes or field trips
- Pet care
- Visiting Zoos or Botanical Gardens
- Visiting Museums of Natural History
- Classifying Information
- Labeling Objects

Naturalist students will enjoy geography, topography, astrology, oceanography, meteorology, and other natural phenomena.

Spatial Intelligence

USING YOUR SPATIAL INTELLIGENCE

Creating a Learning Map

From the beginning of the program the use of Learning Maps has been encouraged.

TO DO

CREATE A STRONG VISUAL IMAGE OF WHAT YOU ARE TRYING TO LEARN IN YOUR MIND'S EYE

At the end of this module, make a large Learning Map that summarizes all that you have learned until now. You will be able to add further information as you read on.

Create sketches or flow charts when problem solving. Many mathematical concepts are easier to solve when you find a way to diagram them. Use symbols instead of words. Color-code your work.

Create an Image

Create a strong visual image of what you are trying to learn in your mind's eye. Imagine watching a TV documentary about the subject you are learning.

To really understand a process, envision yourself as part of the process. If learning about a printed circuit board, for example, see yourself as electricity winding your way through the complex maze to the perfect outcome.

Kinesthetic Intelligence

USING YOUR KINESTHETIC INTELLIGENCE

Role-Play

Being physically involved in the learning allows you to turn theory into more memorable procedural knowledge.

Role-playing helps in the exploration of a new approach or skill while in a safe and controlled environment. Taking on different parts allows you to see the same subject from a different perspective.

> WRITING IS A PHYSICAL EXERCISE THAT TAKES PLACE UNCONSCIOUSLY

For example, people will learn more about the importance of easy access for the disabled by trying to negotiate a building in a wheelchair, or by wearing a blindfold while going from one class to another.

Acting out words and phrases when you are learning a foreign language is very effective, because you physically register the language in your memory.

The Power of Writing

The Power of Writing

Writing is a physical exercise that is called an idiomotor response. It is an action that takes place unconsciously. People do not think of each letter as it is written; they just write.

It should be no surprise, therefore, that when something is written, it is easier to remember. A physical element, sight, and sound have been added. Information was stored and assimilated in the subconscious mind.

Sort your thoughts

Create 3" x 5" cards of the key learning points. Sort them out in a logical order. Carry the flash cards with you and revise with them as new information warrants.

You can also color code the cards and tape them up in your study area. Every time you see the cards, the information will be reinforced.

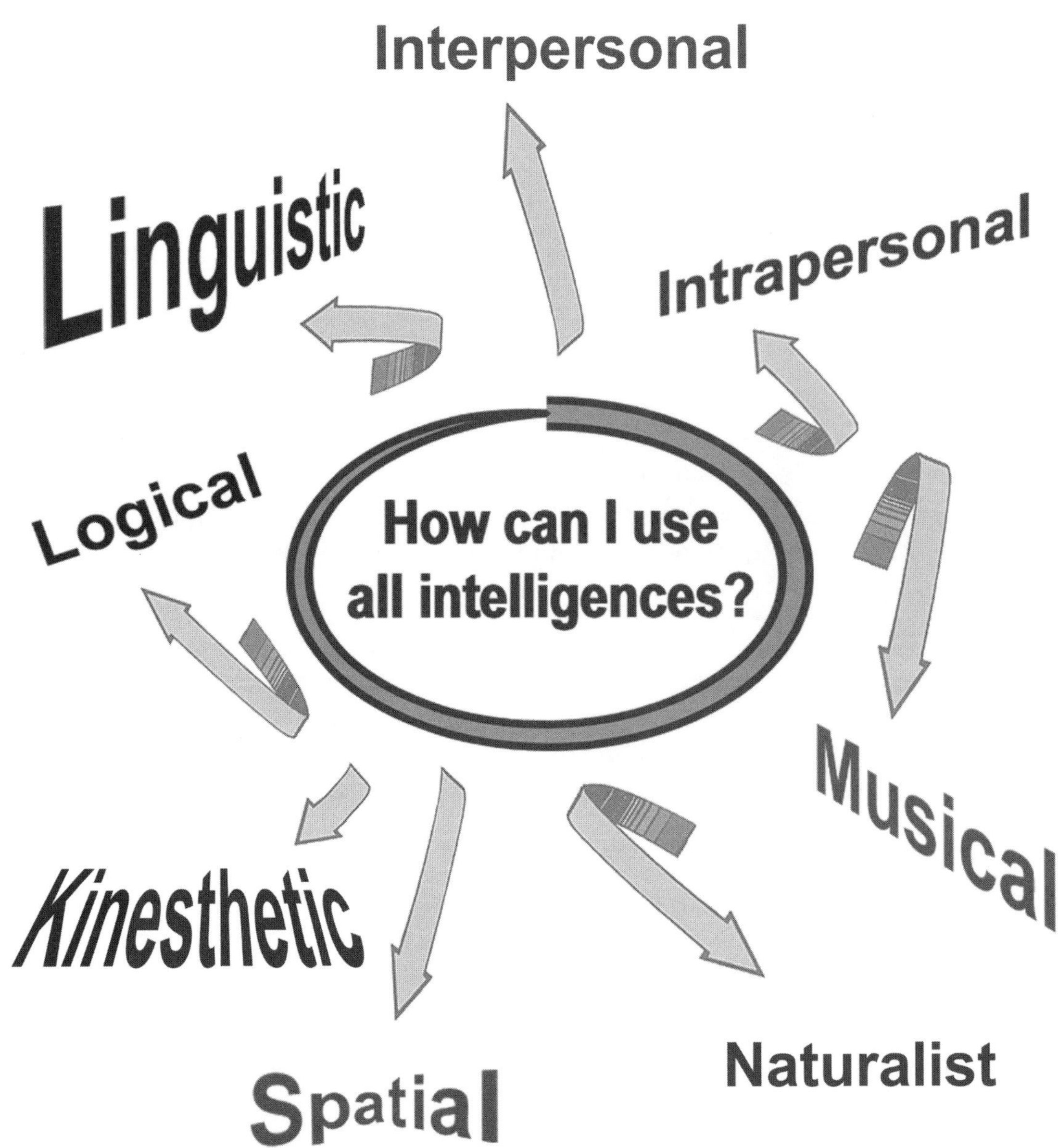
Interpersonal
Intrapersonal
Linguistic
Logical
How can I use all intelligences?
Musical
Kinesthetic
Spatial
Naturalist

INDIVIDUAL PRIORITIES

As a student, be aware that there is the tendency for teachers to use certain intelligences more than others. The **bad news** is that most formal education is conducted in the Logical (Mathematical) and Linguistic modalities. The other intelligences are missed. If you do not fall into one group or both groups when in school, you will probably struggle with certain subjects or maybe all subjects.

Accelerated Learning uses all eight intelligences

The good news: Accelerated Learning uses all eight intelligences. This allows you, the learner, to absorb information according to personal learning style preference and individual order of intelligences.

Using all of the intelligences also allows you to **Express Your Knowledge** based on your innate skill as well as structured required skills. You, for example, may prefer to use your Kinesthetic Intelligence. The teacher, however, may give you a Logical, Linguistic test to take. Your job is to convert from your intelligence to another appropriate to the task.

Take some time to figure out your Intelligences preferences.

Think of your most difficult subject and answer again.

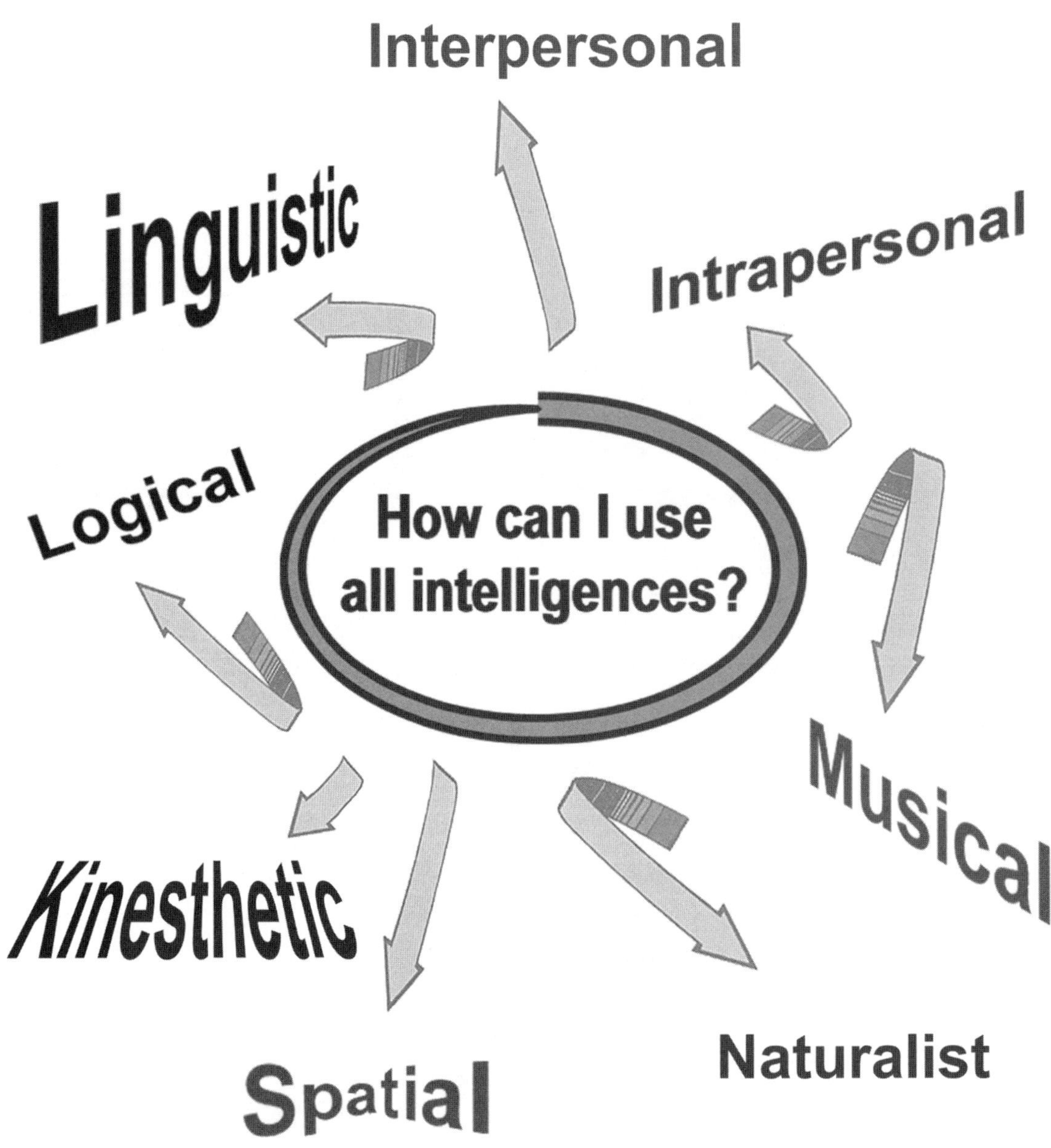

Show You Know Through Practice

This practice or testing stage of your learning should be anticipated as a chance to evaluate how well you are doing. Feedback establishes areas where more work is needed.

You will never know if you have learned something unless you put it to use. But before you put it to use, it is important to practice and express your new knowledge in a "safe" and controlled environment rather than in a real-life situation or a final examination.

Testing Yourself

You are your own best judge. Develop the skill of critiquing your own work to assess how well you are progressing. In traditional education, "tests" are often created so that a certain number of "failures" occur. Failure is expected. If everyone passes then it is thought that the test was too easy!

Accelerated Learning does not plan for failures this way. Everyone can learn according to individualized Learning, Organization and Assimilation styles. Test yourself when you feel ready and want feedback on how much you really know.

Learning that you actually know something is sometimes more important than learning something new!

CATCH YOURSELF DOING THINGS RIGHT

Tests allow you to enhance, adjust or correct what you do not know after discovering the knowledge gaps. Many times, however, learning that you actually know something is often more important than learning something new.

Catching yourself doing things right also reinforces the assimilation process and helps boost your confidence for the next round of learning.

Already in this program you have been assessing your own progress through the "Self-Assessment" exercises at the end of each module. Testing your knowledge is a vital part of learning. How do you know you can do something unless you actually try?

Test yourself with one of the following techniques:

- **Learning Maps**
- **Flash Cards**
- **Imagination**
- **Learning Together**
- **Tell or Teach**
- **Role Play**

Learning Maps

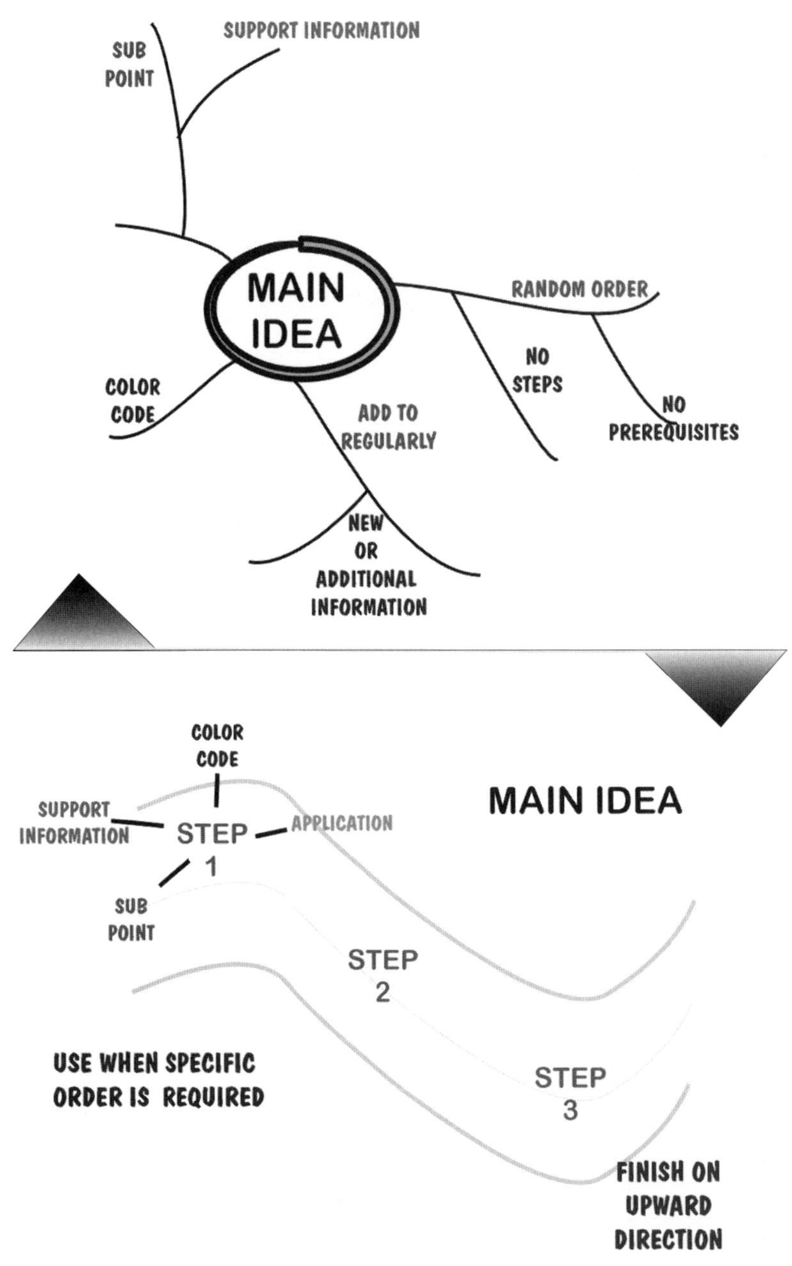

LEARNING MAPS

Learning Maps made during the Intake and Real Meaning Modules make great test-yourself-tools. Take a clean sheet of paper and try to redraw your map from memory.

The color and layout used in your original will help you remember where different branches are on your map. When you have completed your new map, check it against your original.

The areas you duplicated are obviously those you have already committed to memory. You may find there are blank areas where your recall failed temporarily. The blanks merely show the topics where more work is required. You cannot "fail" since you are simply assessing how well you are doing.

Note: Some learning will lend itself to drawing a flowchart of the information as a test of how well you have done. This is merely a variation of the Learning Map concept.

Flashcards are ideal for testing:

- Vocabulary
- Steps in a process
- Procedure
- Definitions
- New foreign words

FLASHCARDS

Flashcards are ideal for testing vocabulary, steps in a process, procedure, definitions or new foreign words. On one side of the Flash Card print the name of the target information. On the reverse, print the description of the key concept. Test yourself from both perspectives.

When learning the steps in a process or a procedure, put each step on a Flash Card and test whether you can get them in the correct order.

TO DO

PLAY "PAIRS" USING FLASH CARDS

Play "pairs" using flash cards. Each card has one half of the equation; i.e., a definition, formula, translated word, etc. These cards are laid out on a table and you try and match the two halves to form the complete answer.

The pairing technique is great for learning foreign words and their meanings or scientific symbols and the compounds to which they refer.

If possible, have a picture on one side of the card instead of a word. Matching the picture to the definition has more impact on learning and memory.

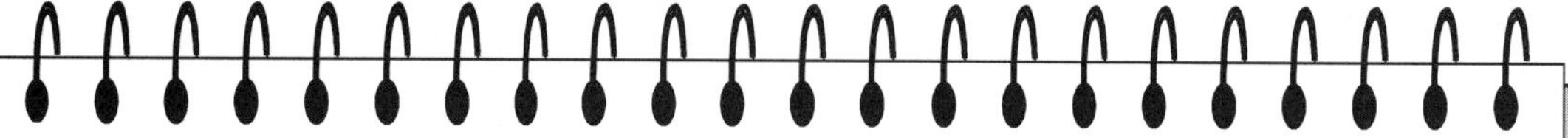

Select any subject.
List or draw what you...

HEAR	SEE	SMELL	FEEL	TASTE

IMAGINATION

In your mind, imagine what you have just learned. Make sure the situation you are imagining is colorful and as real as possible. What do you hear? See? Smell? Feel? Taste? Make yourself part of the action and see yourself completing the task you have learned.

TO DO

MAKE YOURSELF PART OF THE ACTION AND SEE YOURSELF COMPLETING THE TASK YOU HAVE LEARNED

If you are speaking, what are you saying and how are you saying it? Is your presentation factual and direct or are you emotional and animated? This is a great technique to use in a speech class or as a member of a debate club.

LEARNING TOGETHER

If you have a partner learning with you, test each other. Not only do you have chance to "Show You Know", but you will also learn from your partner. Together, you will both have a better learning experience.

Working with someone else gives valuable insight into how a different learning style would tackle the learning task. You will observe the application of alternative strategies. Add these strategies to your repertoire.

Make yourself part of the action and see yourself

completing the task you have learned

TELL OR TEACH

Turn your learning maps or notes into words and express your learning to another person. This really tests how well you have understood the concepts.

Your partner need not be learning with you. In fact, a person who has no knowledge of your subject will pose some great questions that you will need to answer simply and comprehensively.

If the person being taught is struggling with your explanation, you may be forced to use an intelligence that is different than your preferred intelligence. Figure out the intelligence the listener is using and try explaining the information with that particular intelligence.

What subjects could I easily teach?

____

____

____

What subjects would I need to research before teaching others?

____

____

____

Select a famous person you would like to meet. Imagine asking questions. Guess how that person would answer?

ROLE PLAY

A partner is preferable for role-playing. Multiple partners are even better. Two of the participants act out the scenario and the third watches, making notes and offering constructive ideas on how the role-play was conducted.

If you do not have a partner, you can still role-play. Do not just imagine; act out. Play both or multiple parts. Use emotion and emphasis. Critique yourself as you go.

What can I do to test myself?

____

____

____

A whole series of small rights

will make up one BIG right

OVERLAPPING INFORMATION

As you may have noticed, there is a significant overlap between the Assimilation Preferences and the Intelligences. As mentioned earlier, none of the preferences work in isolation.

The good news is that the more Learning Styles you try with different Organization Preferences, the easier it will be to intake information. Once the information is in and you begin to create Real Meaning through Assimilation, you are also exercising different Intelligences.

When you exercise different Intelligences by Expressing Knowledge, you are also reinforcing the Assimilation process that will in turn impact the Learning Style associated with the information being studied.

Every aspect of your learning will overlap in one fashion or another.

Thomas Edison made thousands of attempts to invent the electric light bulb before he finally succeeded.

When asked about this, his reaction was, "I did not fail thousands of times. I merely discovered thousands of ways NOT to make a light bulb."

STEPPING STONES

It is rare that anyone can get everything right at the first attempt. How long did you spend learning to ride a bicycle? Practice made that possible by retracing the correct memory pathway in the brain and muscle memory in the body.

Falling down when you were first learning to ride did not indicate failure. The fall gives feedback! You recover quickly from the fall and learn from the feedback to adjust the approach before trying again.

Thomas Edison made thousands of attempts to invent the electric light bulb before he finally succeeded. When asked about this, his reaction was, "I did not fail thousands of times. I merely discovered thousands of ways NOT to make a light bulb."

Learning requires the same, sensible attitude as Thomas Edison. Mistakes when practicing should be viewed as valuable feedback in order to review and adjust. Every adjustment is another step closer to successful completion. A whole series of small rights will make up one big right.

Self Assessment

1. I know the foundations for learning and I am prepared to expand the ways I use them. *Yes/No*

2. I am comfortable when I make mistakes. I regard mistakes as useful feedback and vital to help me adjust my approach and learn better. *Yes/No*

3. I understand the need for practice. *Yes/No*

I know how to use the following to test myself:

4. Learning Maps *Yes/No*

5. Flash Cards *Yes/No*

6. Visualization *Yes/No*

7. Learning Together *Yes/No*

8. Tell and Teach *Yes/No*

9. Role Play *Yes/No*

10. I am confident and feel ready to apply my learning in a real situation. *Yes/No*

SUMMARY - MODULE 4

Intelligence is a combination of Assimilation and Output of knowledge. The smartest people in the world live in LLIIMNSK because they use every one of the intelligences described by Howard Gardner.

L - Logical

L - Linguistic

I - Interpersonal

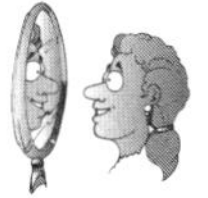
I - Intrapersonal

M - Musical

N - Naturalistic

S - Spatial

K - Kinesthetic

SHOW YOU KNOW BY PRACTICING.

You are your own best judge. There are several ways to test yourself:

Learning Maps

Flash Cards

Visualization

Learning Together

Tell or Teach

Role Play

Stepping Stones lead to success. Mistakes are not stumbling blocks, but are opportunities to step forward toward successful learning.

I Am Ready!

CREATE A LEARNING MAP OF MODULE 4

What else do I need or want to know?

____

Where can I find the information?

____

Whom do I want to ask?

____

MODULE 5

Foundations

Intake Information

Real Meaning

Express Your Knowledge

Use Available Resources

Plan of Action

Teacher
Flip-C
Mentors
USE
Available Resources
Learning Partners
Computers & Internet
BOOK POWER!
SCHOOL
Library
Family & Friends

MODULE 5

U - USE AVAILABLE RESOURCES

Utilize Other People 263
Mentors 265
Teachers or Instructors 265
Learning Partner 265
Family Member or Friend 267
Use Other Resources 267
Use Your New Knowledge 269
Module Five Summary 271

Introduction

This is the stage where you can now apply your new knowledge. Research suggests that when learning something new you should use it within 24 hours for maximum results.

Who do I know could help me expand my learning?

Who can I turn to when I need information related to a specific subject?

What Web Sites besides www.fire-up.com can I use to expand my knowledge?

U - USE AVAILABLE RESOURCES

UTILIZE OTHER PEOPLE

Other people have been where you are going. They too have learned the skill or application you are studying. One last piece of advice before you use your new knowledge is to UTILIZE these people.

Select people you believe are excellent at what they do. Why are they excellent? What do they do right? How can I apply these skills with my current base of knowledge?

The people you select can be mentors, peers, relatives, teachers, or friends. On occasion the person you select could be an historical figure or even a fictional character.

Follow in their footsteps and learn from their experiences. Watch how they perform the task, or read about their application of the knowledge.

If possible ask them to explain their method of application.

If it is not possible to have a face-to-face conversation with the person you have selected, imagine having it. The more ways you look at tackling an activity, the broader your understanding will be.

Mentors

Who do I know that can help me with different subjects?

____

____

____

MENTORS

A mentor is someone who is highly skilled in the area you are learning. Taking their advice will help you avoid any unconsidered pitfalls. Ask them to clarify any areas you still feel unsure of.

If it is applicable, ask if your mentor can accompany you and watch as you complete the task "live". The feedback on how you performed and how things may have been done differently will be invaluable.

If your mentor cannot be with you on your debut, describe your experience to your mentor. Describe how you think it went and ask about any aspects you feel need improvement as well as what you did right.

Teachers or Instructors

Your teacher or instructor is one of the best sources of feedback after you have performed the task. Meet with this person and tell them how you felt you did. Ask them for helpful advice and quiz them about any aspects you feel you need more information about.

Learning Partner

The use and review technique can also be conducted with a partner who is applying the same or similar knowledge. Debriefing together means you can learn from each other's experience.

Other resources

Where can I go to learn more about specific subjects?

Family Member or Friend

If you don't have a mentor, teacher or learning partner, share your experience with a family member or friend. To tell someone just how the exercise went, and where you felt you could have improved, is a valuable way for you to think through, review and adjust.

Use Other Resources

In addition to people, look at other resources that will help you perfect your learning such as books and the Internet. Never before has so much knowledge been freely available as now through the Internet.

Additional information and helpful tips about your subject can be found by searching the Worldwide Web. With so much information available at your fingertips, however, it is important to be selective and disciplined.

Make a plan (described in the next module) for subject related material. As you find documents, ask yourself "Does this really apply to what I want to know?" When you find useful information remember to bookmark or record the address of the page so you can refer to it again easily.

Use Your Knowledge Immediately

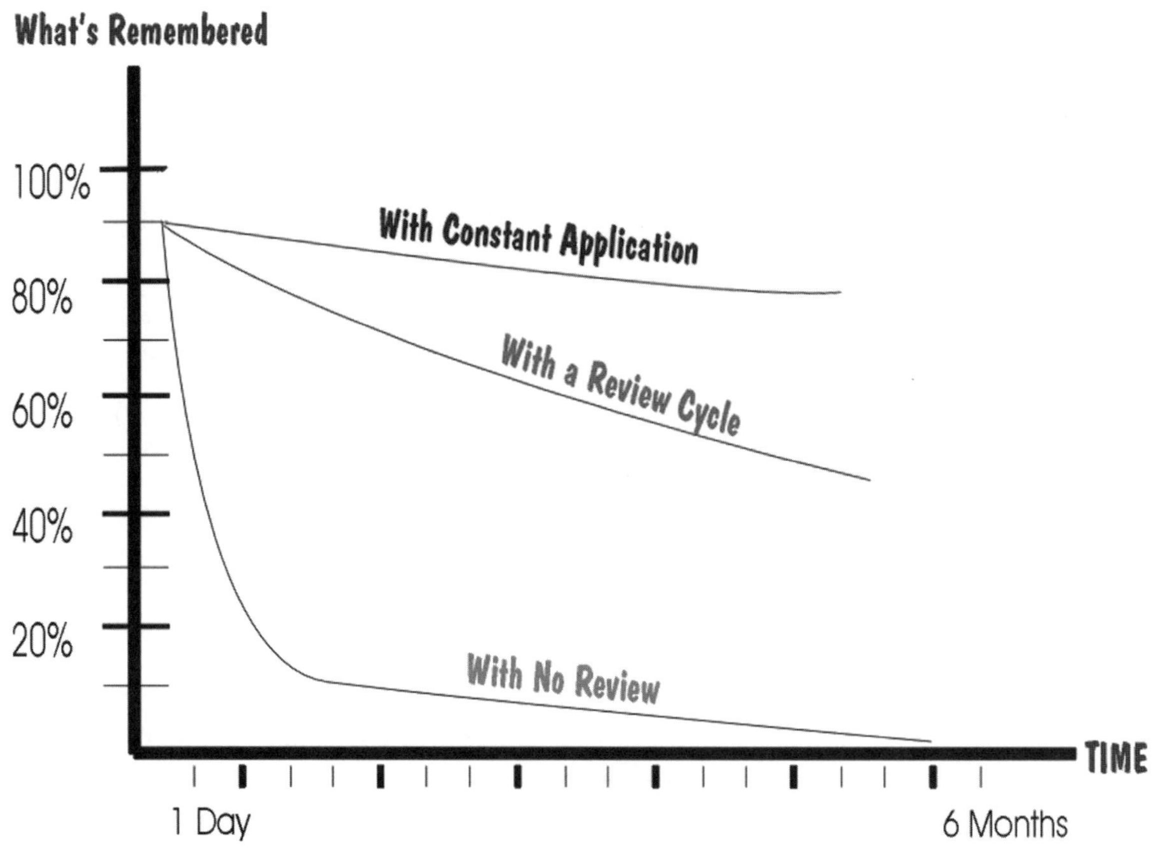

Remember what you learn

USE YOUR NEW KNOWLEDGE

Blend your new knowledge with other learning. If you are taking a class in typing and a class in history, type something about your latest history lesson.

- Make short reminder notes.
- Draw a flow chart of a new method you have learned.
- Place the notes in your study area. You will now have a visual reminder of the new procedure that will become reinforced every time you see it.

Use the same information in different ways. The more variety you have with a subject, the more brain connections are created. The more connections you have, the greater the opportunity to recall the same information from multiple stimuli.

Self Assessment

1. I understand the need to use my new information immediately.
2. When utilizing other's skills, I understand what a mentor is and how the mentor concept works.
3. When utilizing other's skills, I understand the importance of feedback from teachers and instructors.
4. When utilizing other's skills, I understand why friends and family can be so important to my continuing development.
5. When utilizing other's skills, I understand why learning partners can give me a different point of view.
6. I understand how to find information from other sources.
7. I understand that mistakes are part of learning and they are moving me closer to success.
8. I have used creative ways to intake this information.
9. I have practiced the different Assimilation preferences.
10. I have made a Learning Map of this module.

SUMMARY - MODULE 5

Using your knowledge is vital to strengthening the memory traces and expanding your dendrite network. In other words, you become a smarter, faster learner.

Utilize other people. Your selection can be mentors, peers, relatives, teachers, co-workers, managers, or friends. They can be alive today, historical figures, public figures or even fictional characters.

Follow in their footsteps and learn from their experiences.

Utilize other sources. Do not accept everything at face value. There are times to pull out the Contrary Assimilator role to double check the sources.

Use your knowledge as quickly as possible. If you recall from Module One, you put information in a box and store it in the basement when it is no longer being used. More boxes will get piled in front of and on top of the first box. The more boxes that are on the pile, the tougher it is to get to the first box.

On the other hand, using the information in a particular box keeps it in a convenient spot. The easier the information is to get to the more it will be used.

CREATE A LEARNING MAP OF MODULE 5

What else do I need or want to know?

___

Where can I find the information?

___

Whom can I ask?

___

MODULE 6

Foundations

Intake Information

Real Meaning

Express Your Knowledge

Use Available Resources

Plan of Action

Intake
Information
Real Meaning
New Knowledge
Current Knowledge
Foundations
PLAN OF ACTION
Express
Your
Knowledge
Use
Available
Resources

MODULE 6

P - PLAN OF ACTION

Elements of Planning - Overview 277
- Assessment 281
- The Mission Statement 285
- Goals - Be S.M.A.R.T. 291
- Responsibilities 293
- Timing 293
- Action Items 293
- Flexibility 295

Summary - Module 6 301

Introduction

Up to now you have discovered your learning style, your preferences for assimilating information and your primary intelligence. This final module is an equally important element in your future learning. In order to put the information into practice, you must have a plan.

In this module, the seven key elements of planning and goal setting will be covered. It will then be important for you to take the time to develop a plan that is realistic and personalized to your own style.

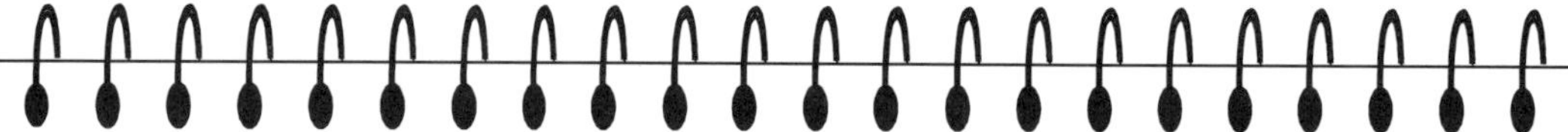

What do I know about planning?

Where am I now with my learning plan?

Can I establish a Mission for my current and future Learning?

Have I set SMART goals?

Although I know that I am completely responsible for learning, who else should be involved for specific subjects? (See Module 5)

Have I set attainable deadlines for my learning plan?

What steps have I taken to reach my goals?

Is my plan flexible in case something goes wrong or finish early?

P - PLAN OF ACTION

ELEMENTS OF PLANNING

Overview

You now understand the Foundations of Accelerated Learning. You can Intake and organize the information in a way that best suits your personal style. You can create Real Meaning through a process of assimilation. Expressing Your Knowledge is now easy because you understand how to maximize all of your intelligences. And, to Use other sources is the method you will include to expand and solidify your knowledge.

The next step is to Plan what you want to learn.

This module covers the elements of planning. Several of these elements have been touched on throughout the program. Study "goals" and study "time" management is part of the planning process. Also the "flexibility" to adapt to the different teaching styles and classroom environments is important in establishing the learning technique you will be using.

The seven elements of planning will complete the picture.

Planning

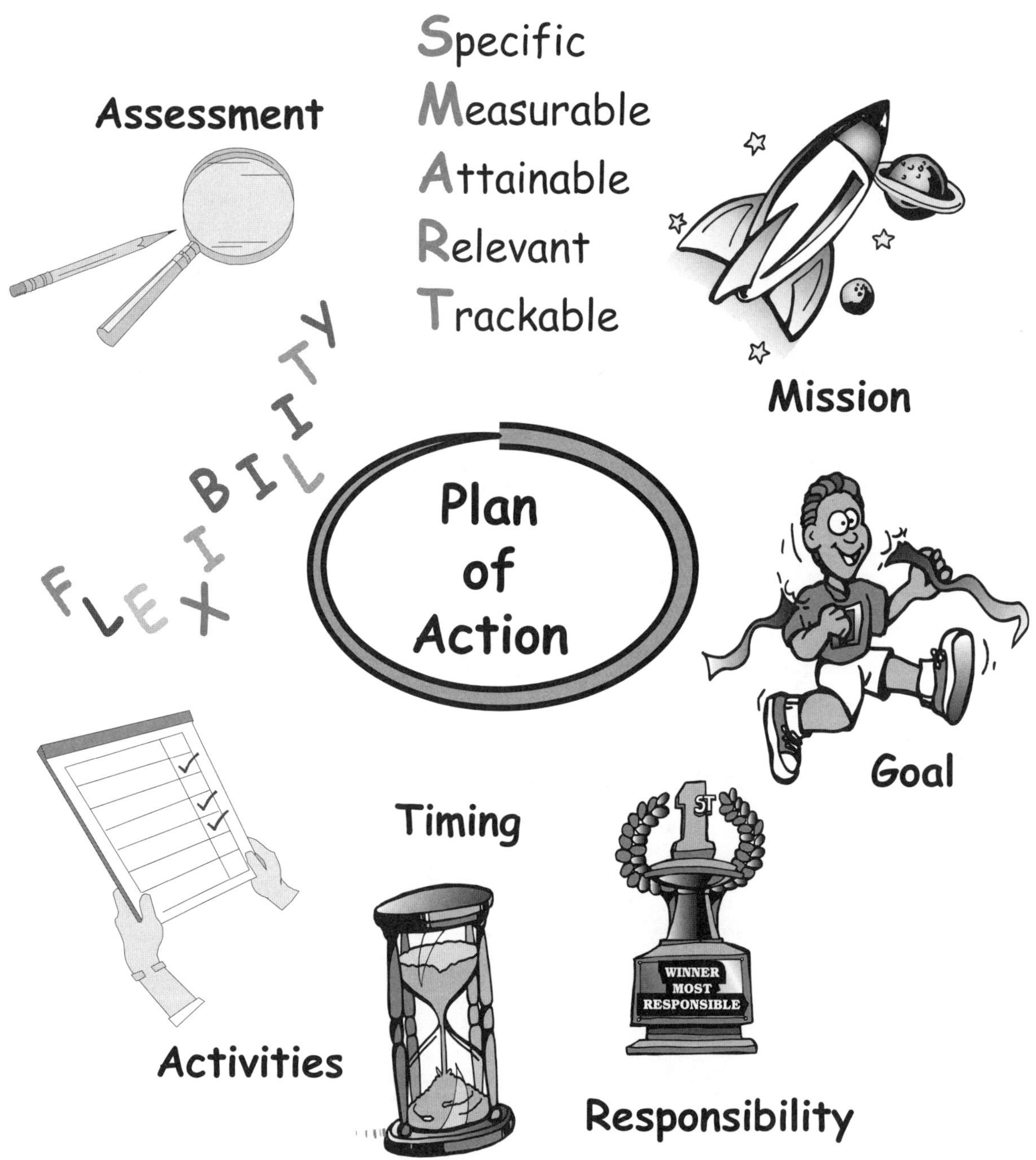
Specific
Measurable
Attainable
Relevant
Trackable
Assessment
Mission
FLEXIBILITY
Plan of Action
Goal
Timing
1ST
WINNER
MOST
RESPONSIBLE
Activities
Responsibility

The definition of planning is the process of determining how a desired objective will be reached, and what will be required along the way. It follows that a good plan requires these seven elements:

1. Assessment
2. Mission
3. Goals
4. Responsibility
5. Timing
6. Action Items
7. Flexibility

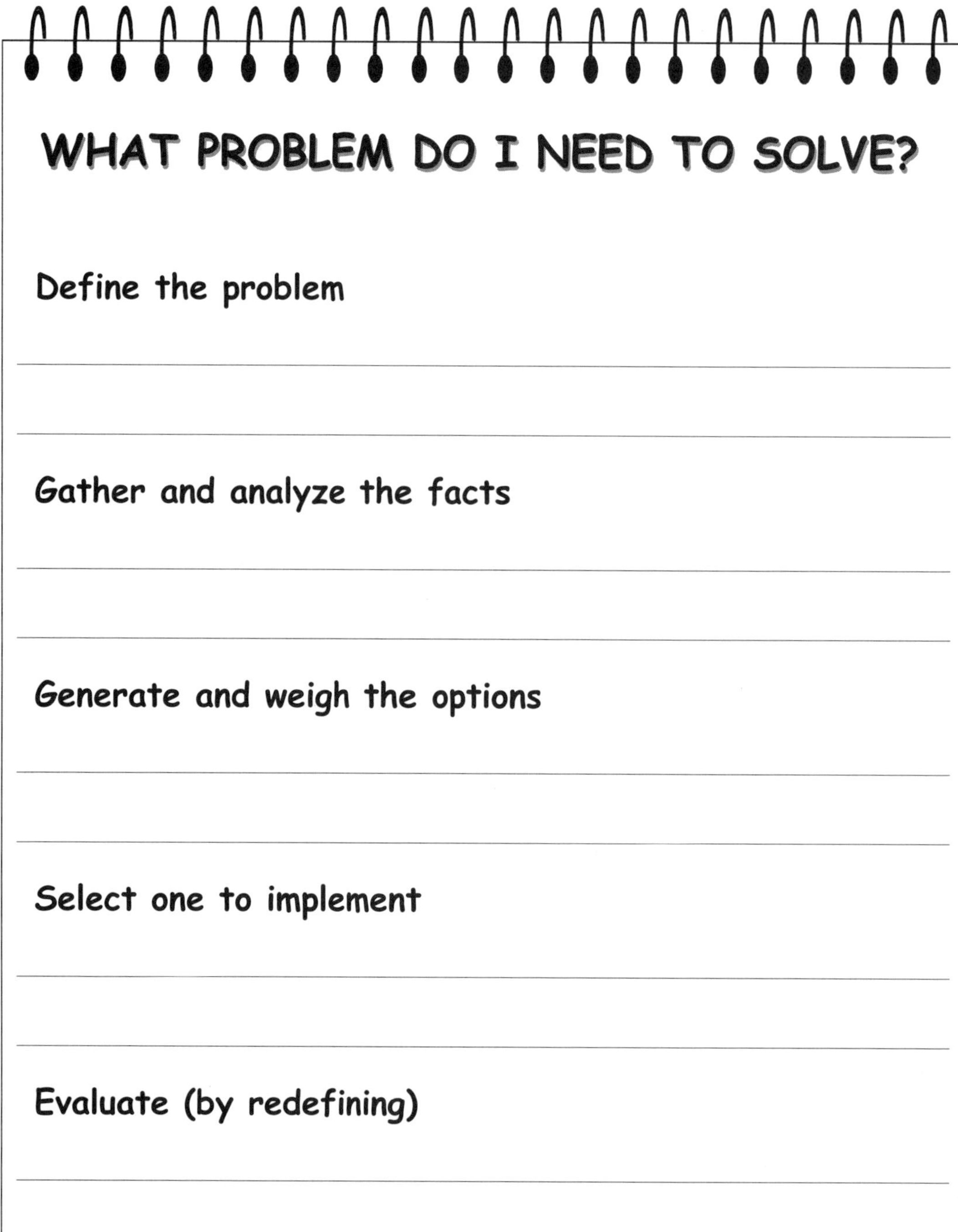
WHAT PROBLEM DO I NEED TO SOLVE?
Define the problem
Gather and analyze the facts
Generate and weigh the options
Select one to implement
Evaluate (by redefining)

1. Assessment (Where is the starting point?)

Accurate assessment is the most vital point in planning. In order to know what direction to take to reach a specific objective, planning strategy requires a starting point.

Educated Guesses

Numerical assessments, although tedious, are easy because of the associated objective nature. The more defined a subject is, the less confusion there is related to the interpretation of the subject.

Assessing external influences and internal capabilities are more subjective and create wide latitude for interpretation. Therefore, the more subjective an assessment is, the more models are needed. Incorporate any tools that increase objectivity.

If, for example, you were to teach another person how to make a decision, what process would be described? Most have difficulty answering that because decision-making is an unconscious thought process. The answer is "You just do it".

The problem is that "just doing it" does not really teach the model.

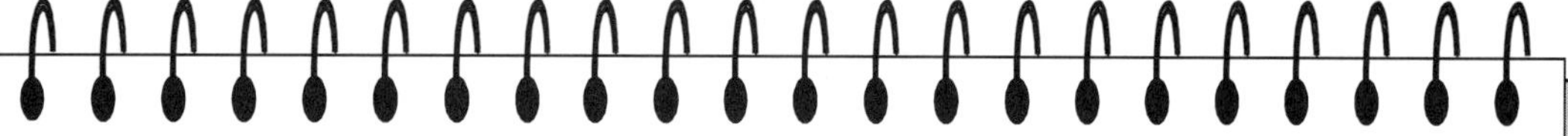

WHAT PROBLEM DO I NEED TO SOLVE?

Define the problem

Gather and analyze the facts

Generate and weigh the options

Select one to implement

Evaluate (by redefining)

The Decision Making Model

1. Define the Problem
2. Gather and Analyze the Facts
3. Generate Options and Weigh Those Options
4. Select an Option and Implement
5. Evaluate

At Noontime, for example, you define the problem: "I need to eat lunch." So you go to a restaurant and get a menu or gather the facts. You analyze the menu. Your options are "salad bar" or "double-chili cheeseburger". You select the double-chili cheeseburger and order (implement the selected option). After two hours of indigestion (evaluate the selected option), you eliminate the double-chili cheeseburger as any future option.

This is how decisions are made. The Decision-Making Model can be used at anytime. It is especially helpful during the planning process.

The clearer you are with your assessment of yourself and your situation, the better your plan will be.

The Mission Statement

NOTE:
To help with your learning mission, return to the hot air balloon. Review the information. You may want to change your benefits and issues.

2. The Mission Statement (Why?)

The Mission is a guiding star or your main purpose in life. The mission statement is the "Granddaddy" of all goals. A mission is a compass that gives the direction to stay the course.

Mission statements are generally written for customers or stockholders of major corporations. They are generic and include grandiose terminology. Your mission statement, however, needs to be personalized. By re-framing the definition of a mission statement, the process becomes definable.

The Mission is what you want others to *ideally* say about the way you conduct your life.

- Ideally, what do you want your fellow classmates to say about you as a peer?
- Ideally, what do you want the teachers and school administrators to say about you as a student and as a person?
- Ideally, what would you like your friends to say about you?
- If you were in an organized group or an athletic team, ideally, what would you like your team mates to say?

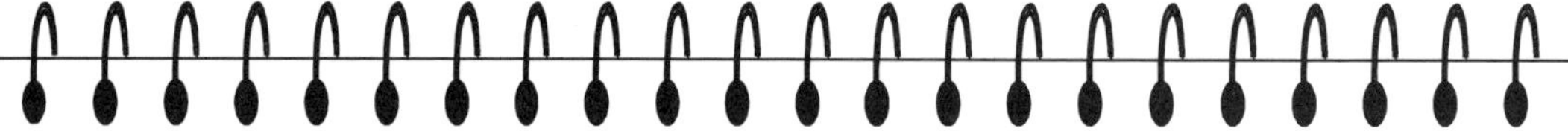

Ideally, what words would you like to hear from people in each group?

PEERS	TEACHERS	FRIENDS	TEAMMATES

The Process

The answer to these questions is the means to generating a Mission. Organize the key words and common terms from each group into a paragraph format. Place the mission statement in a location that is easily accessible. The objective of a mission statement is to maintain focus on the ultimate outcome.

In the columns on the opposite page, brainstorm words or key ideas that would be ideal from each of the groups.

Now that the key thoughts have been generated, a pattern of words will appear that are common to each column. Use those words first to develop a paragraph or two that would make up the initial mission statement.

Once the first draft is written, blend the words that are exclusive to each column into the statement to make it more complete. If necessary to further customize the Mission Statement, add more related columns to address individual needs.

Since the Mission Statement represents the ideal, then it is important to constantly move toward that ideal. Keep the Mission Statement in a place that is readily visible; i.e., a daytimer, desk, or a visor in the car. Review the statement regularly. Remember that the Mission Statement is for motivation and focus.

Today is a beautiful day. The sun is shining brightly. Children are playing in the park. They are very loud. My Uncle is coming right now to meet me. We are going to see a strange movie about two dogs and a cat trying to save their owner from the bad guys.

There are six Relative Terms in this story. Can you pick them out?

1 ____________________________________

2 ____________________________________

3 ____________________________________

4 ____________________________________

5 ____________________________________

6 ____________________________________

beautiful, brightly, very loud, Uncle (is a relative), strange, bad guys

Relative Terminology

Relative terminology is any term that can be defined based on a person's paradigms, prejudices or preferences (see Analytical Mind). A relative word is what you **believe** the word means.

The word "two", for example, is a concrete term. If someone says to you, "How many pencils do you have?" and you say, "I have two, fine pencils", everyone will understand exactly the number of pencils you have.

On the other hand, what does "fine" mean? Does it mean, "thin"? "excellent"? "satisfactory"? or, is it the name of the pencil company? If a person has to guess what "fine" means, that person is defining the word based on what the individual's perception or belief is. The other person's answer may or may not agree with what you meant when you said "I have two, fine pencils".

The word professional is an example. One person can interpret the word "professional" completely different than another. One may say professional is being paid for a specific skill as in a professional athlete. Another may say professional means someone has a high degree of integrity or knowledge or leadership.

Mission Statements are typically laced with relative terminology. Mission Statements are, therefore, interpreted by the reader causing relative terms to be ideal for the Mission Statement.

Because of the interpretation factor, Personal Mission Statements should only be shared with those who will support the efforts to achieve that mission and should be shared with those who are part of the mission.

Goals are set too high and too low.
Goals are secret - no one can know.
Goals are boring and hard to explain,
It is easier to sit, sigh and complain.
Interesting though, as you sit and you sigh,
It is the people with goals who are passing you by.

Unknown

The Mission Statement is the overall direction. Goals are the shorter-term direction to move toward the mission. At any given time, a plan may include several goals.

3. Goals (What needs to be accomplished?)

BE SMART

Specific

Measurable

Attainable

Relevant

Trackable

Regardless of the types of goals you are establishing, the goals must be **SMART**.

Specific goals are definable. There are no "gray" areas or room for interpretation. All words used are concrete in nature; i.e., make the "Dean's List" for academic achievement.

Measurable goals have a beginning and an end. There is a very distinct line to cross. Therefore, at the end of a specific time, it will be obvious if the goal has been reached or not. If the goal was missed, the measurement will know the short fall exactly. If the goal was exceeded, the measurement will indicate the exact overage.

Attainable goals are real-world goals that push the comfort zone outward. (See Analytical Mind). Some people set goals too high just to set themselves up for failure and the ensuing sympathy. Other people set goals too low because they do not want to bother or they want to stay in their rut. Attainable goals are balanced AND challenging.

Relevant goals are directly related to the mission and give meaning to the goal. If the goal does not mean anything, the intensity will be low and the dedication to the goal will be lacking.

Trackable goals have a series of checkpoints along the way. Trackable means that if there is a 90-day goal, the 89th day is too late to determine if the goal is going to be made. When goals are trackable, follow up on related activities becomes easier and much less stressful.

Responsibility

Timing

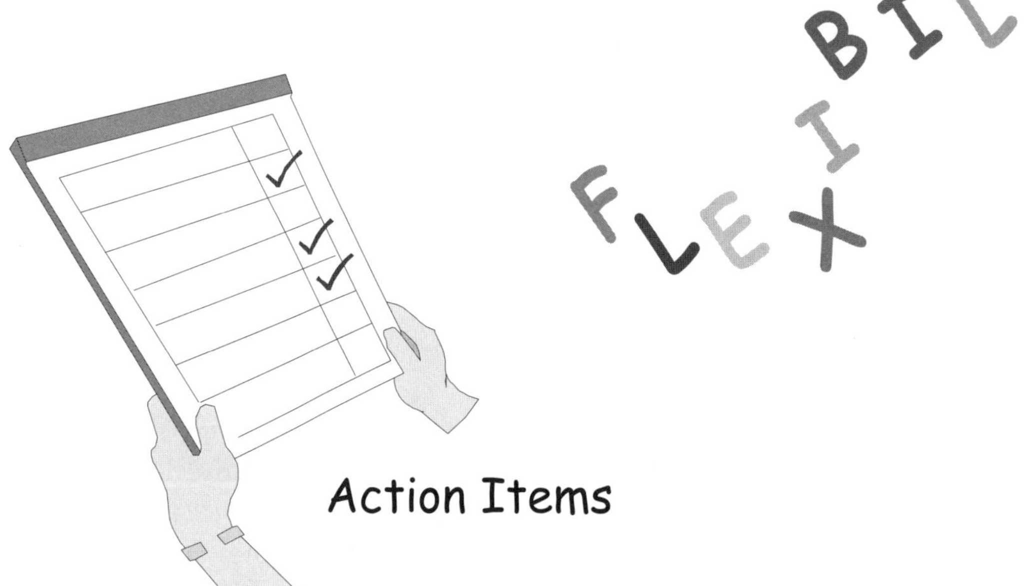

Action Items

4. Responsibilities (Who is required to carry out planned tasks?)

- Determine what assistance is required from others. (See Use Available Resources)
- Make sure the people involved are fully aware of their part of the plan

5. Timing (When is the plan to be completed?)

- Establish a realistic forecast
- Set scheduled starting and completion dates
- Define checkpoints that will determine progress

6. Action Items (How are you going to get there?)

This is the to-do list. By listing every action item, focus can be maintained. A list with appropriate timing allows for easy follow up with each of those items.

To develop a plan, ask yourself:

Who?

What?

When?

Where?

Why?

How?

and be prepared to be

FLEXIBLE

7. Flexibility (Re-plan)

- Was your planning research sufficient?
- What additional information would have been helpful?
- Do you have a plan for future information gathering and assimilation?
- How can the process be improved?

Murphy is alive and well. Murphy's law says "If anything can go wrong, it will". Stay prepared for changes and adjustments to the system. When focused on the Mission and the Goals, re-planning is easy.

Although there have been hundreds of books written on planning, the process is really very simple. Every time a plan is developed, answers to the following questions will make it difficult to fail:

Who?

What?

When?

Where?

Why?

How?

FLEXIBILITY

Attaining Your Goals

DO NOT CHANGE YOUR GOALS. Once the goals are set, keep focused on getting there. If you constantly change your goals, two things happen:

1. **The goals will be meaningless.** If you know you can get off the hook by merely changing the goal, the importance of goal setting is lost. If your goal was too high and you miss it, you will learn to be a better goal-setter in the future. The same applies to a goal that is too low. If you blow by the goal, you have not pushed the fences of your comfort zone out. It's no fun playing a game if the game is too easy.

2. **You will not know if you ever reach a goal**. Changing the goal is like moving the finish line in a race. You thought you knew where the finish line was when the race started, but when you get there the line is gone. It is no fun playing a game if the rules change so you cannot win.

There is one last point about planning. Do not get "paralysis by analysis". Go through the process and get started. You can always add additional goals. Your action items are going to be flexible.

There is an old adage in the corporate business world that applies to academic learning as well: **plan your work and work your plan.**

Self Assessment

What have you learned so far?

Throughout this program you have been identifying activities that are compatible with your unique brain. Now it's time to decide just exactly how you learn best and how you can develop those skills further.

Develop a learning map that describes your primary styles and preferences. List the secondary styles that you would be comfortable using. **PLAN** to use the others not listed.

To develop your Plan of Action for the future, answer the following questions based on your experiences so far:

- What motivates me?
- How can I use this in my learning?

1. Different things motivate people. List below the things that are generally important to you.

___

___

___

2. What are my strengths?

___

___

___

3. What are my greatest challenges to learning?

___

___

___

4. After analyzing the facts related to the challenges, what are my options to turn the challenges into opportunities?

___

___

___

5. After prioritizing the options, what **SMART** Goals can I set to maximize my efforts to reach the mission?

____

____

____

6. Who can help?

____

____

____

7. When will I reach these goals?

____

____

____

8. What Action Items must I have to reach the goals?

____

____

____

SUMMARY - MODULE 6

Keep the planning process simple.

To create a powerful plan, just answer a few easy questions:

Where am I now?	**A**ssessment.
Why am I doing what I am doing?	**M**ission.
What exactly do I need to accomplish?	**S**MART Goals.
Who else needs to be involved in this process?	**R**esponsibility.
When is the goal going to be met?	**T**iming.
How am I going to get there?	**A**ction Items.

Once the plan is set, be prepared to make adjustments to your action items.

Flexibility is important when attempting to reach your goals.

BOOK SUMMARY

The summary for this book is actually up to you.

Are you ready to
FIRE-UP Your Learning?

- Create a summary learning map of everything you have learned in this program.
- Start to apply the easiest concept and then try the next easiest and so on.
- Choose the method most compatible with your style. Then, try a new way of learning.

FIRE-UP Your Learning

and

Learn Easily for a Lifetime!

Test Taking Strategies

FIRE-UP Your Learning is a web-supported program. You can view or download a detailed version of the following information on test-taking strategies.

Test Taking Strategies

For more information on test taking strategies log on to: www.fire-up.com

Real Meaning

F·I·R·E-U·P

Plan
of Action

TEST TAKING STRATEGIES

The FIRE-UP system should already have you prepared. As a quick review:

FOUNDATION

You have a tremendous potential to learn. You have around one hundred billion brain cells that can have ten thousand branches (dendrites) communicating with thousands of other cells. It is not a matter of IF you can learn, it is a matter of HOW!

INTAKE INFORMATION

Anything that impacts one or more of the five senses is a "learning style" (see "learning style - intake"). The more learning styles that you can use to learn something, the greater the chance that the same information will be stored in different parts of the brain.

REAL MEANING

Once the information is in and it is organized, the **new data must be attached to something you already know**. It is similar to linking a new computer file with a file already on the hard drive. Although you can retrieve individually stored files, it is easier to find a file when it is attached to or directly related to a specific folder.

EXPRESS YOUR KNOWLEDGE

By teaching, you are also learning.

USE AVAILABLE RESOURCES

Get another point of view on the subject being taught. By looking at the same thing in different ways, different links get created.

PLAN OF ACTION

Planning and time management are vital to successful test taking. Planning is simply the process of determining how a desired goal will be reached and what will be needed.

TEST ANXIETY

Test anxiety is labeled an anxiety because it is mostly an imagined fear. Generally speaking, fear is reality based while an anxiety is an imagined fear. The physical and emotional result can be the same. If a person has a "fear of flying" but that person has never flown, then the person is said to have a severe anxiety. If, on the other hand, the same person had been in a plane accident, the fear is now reality based.

Test anxieties can range from mild to severe The anxiety can be chronic - occurring at every test no matter how important the test is. Or, test anxiety can be acute - only occurring for certain tests or types of tests.

Mild test anxiety is actually good news. The Limbic System in the brain's center stimulates the flow of adrenaline. Although a few "butterflies" in your stomach may be present, this creates a hyper-awareness resulting in a more focused approach on the task of completing the test. Concentration, which reduces interference, is also at a higher state.

Severe test anxiety is not that common. When it does strike, however, significant mental and physical distress can occur. Ulcers, vomiting, fainting, extended periods of weeping, and acute depression can be the ultimate result.

For most who experience test anxiety beyond the mild level, "high anxiety" sets in. High anxiety can cause the brain to shut down temporarily. How many times have you been in a test and cannot think of the answer? As soon as you walk out of the testing room, all of the answers just pop into your mind.

Under high anxiety, the chemical and hormonal makeup of the brain will block the ability to recall certain information. The lack of recall creates more stress that slows the brain's ability even further. As soon as the test is over and the related stress is done, the brain re-activates and all of the answers become clear.

This text focuses on high anxiety. Mild test anxiety, as mentioned is good. If you suffer from severe test anxiety, do yourself a favor and seek out a specialist who can counsel you. Books on the subject may help, but talking the problem over with a professional who truly understands your issues will be much more powerful.

Causes of Test Anxiety

The anxiety is often caused by lack of preparation that stimulates an uncomfortable feeling associated with the unknown. The FIRE-UP system will not only get you prepared, it will boost your confidence going into the test.

Risk associated with the test can impact the level of anxiety. The risks can vary and be real reasons, such as:

- Failing to qualify for the college you want to attend
- Failing to qualify for a job you want
- Losing a job or license
- Not receiving a privilege (driver's license)
- The chance that you may need to repeat an important or expensive course

Negative self-talk can sometimes be worse than reality based issues.

- Setting yourself up for failure – "I am too stupid to get this stuff".
- Disappointing yourself – "I knew I would never pass this test".
- Disappointing others – "My parents are really going to be upset if I don't ace this test".
- Projecting the worst-case scenario – "I'll never get out of this hole if I don't do well on this test".
- Blaming people or circumstances for your failure – "I can't study with everyone bothering me all the time"; "If I had a better computer, I could get higher grades".

Preventing (or reducing) Test Anxiety

- Use the FIRE-UP system to prepare
- Develop a test-day routine
- Get a good night's sleep
- Avoid Cramming – Relax and Review
- Eat light and right
- Use positive affirmations
- Imagine Success
- Avoid artificial stimulants

Proactive Prevention

Eliminate the Negative Emotions

On a piece of paper, write out the absolute worse thing that could happen if you do not do well on the test. Just below, in another paragraph, write down what actually might happen in reality. One way to handle the second paragraph is to answer the question: "So what?" "So what if I do fail? Will the worst thing really happen?"

In the third paragraph, write out what you can do to minimize the potentially negative situation. What is the goal or key idea that will significantly reduce the worst-case situation?

Roadblocks and Solutions

1. Divide a piece of paper in half lengthwise. On the left side of the paper, write down all of the barriers that could prevent you from reaching the goal of achieving maximum results on the test. On the right side of the paper, write down solutions to those potential problems.

2. Go back and prioritize the list. Set your solution plan into action. This may mean you need to talk to other people for help or to rearrange a meeting. It may require some creative thinking to generate a solution.

3. If you cannot think of a solution immediately, move to the next item on your priority list. Generally one of the other solutions will apply or can be adapted to other barriers.

4. Start action immediately. If you find that you want to delay, go back and review the list. Break the solutions into smaller pieces. Start with an action item that can be done quickly and that will be easy to complete Immediately move to the next item on your list.

5. Check off the solutions as you complete them. Get friends or family involved with action items that could move you forward. Make sure to thank the helpers once the job is complete. Keep in mind that any assigned tasks are still your responsibility and you must follow up. Do not blame someone else for not completing a task.

Example:

Problem:	Solution:
My boss has asked me to work several extra hours this week. This will cut into my study time and my research time.	Create flash cards that I can use to review during breaks and lunch. Have John pick up two books from the Library that I need. See if my sister can type the outline for my paper. I can fill it in later.

No Excuses

Allowing yourself to blame circumstances or others for your problems will only create more problems.

"Relatives came in town and took up my time."

"I got sick just before the test."

"The Teacher didn't explain this very well."

Even though the above statements may be true and real, they are still no excuse. Interruptions and distractions will occur all of the time and at the worst possible time. You must build flexibility in your study plans.

Use the roadblocks and solutions method to find immediate solutions. Learn from the events so that preparation for the next test can take the events into consideration. If the event does not occur, you are ahead of the game.

Test Day

- Get Up Early
- Eat Light and Nutritionally
- Think Positive

Just Before the Test

- Chat with others about anything but the test
- Get your test kit out (pencils, pens, rulers, calculator, etc.)
- Know the rules (time, penalties for guessing, etc.)

The Test

- Handle the Administration (name, course number, etc.)
- Put Your Pencil Down. Take a deep breath and relax. Say to your brain (to yourself), "OK brain, it is time to go find the answers."
- Read through the questions first. This sets your mind up to open and organize the files that you will need.

First Answers First

Begin the test with the easiest part. It is not necessary to answer the questions in order. Only answer the questions that you are sure are right on the first pass. If you can, put a check mark by the ones you think you know, but need to think through.

1. Start at the beginning and go to the questions you are pretty sure you know. Reason the answers. Do not second-guess yourself.

2. Next, go to those questions that you do not think you know. What will have happened by this time, the brain will have had a chance to research those questions. Answers will amazingly show up. If the question is something you have never heard before, skip it.

3. Last, go to the questions that appear to be brand new information. Read the question carefully. The question can give you clues. There may be a word or phrase that was referenced in another question you already answered.

If you indeed have no clue, learn from the experience. Immediately after the test, ask the teacher about the question. Find out what the teacher was looking for in the question. This will help you better understand the teacher and prepare for the next test.

Handing In the Test

When you are finished, hand the test in with confidence and a smile. This is especially true if there are essay questions or formulas on the answer sheet.

Handing in the test with confidence effects two people. First it reinforces the work that you have done to prepare. You can feel good that you gave it your best shot.

Second it affects the teacher. If the teacher believes you are confident, you may be given the benefit of the doubt on some of your answers. If you look totally confused when you hand the test in, the teacher may assume you had no clue what you were really writing. It could make the difference between a B+ and an A.

The Multiple-Choice Test

Most multiple-choice questions require no opinion or interpretation. The questions are objective, not subjective. Essay questions are just the opposite.

Multiple-choice test can require you to:

a) Recall specific information
b) Reason out the "best" answer"
c) Separate one answer from overlapping data
d) All of the above

The answer is d).

When reviewing a multiple-choice question, there are three components to consider:

- Basis - what the question is all about
- Options - the choices you have to answer the question
- Diversions - sets of information designed to divert your attention

The "basis" is what the question is all about. The basis could be a simple as one word or as complex as an entire paragraph. The basis for the question could also be a situation, case or scenario. All three require that the test taker quickly decide what the main point of the description is.

When analyzing a multiple-choice test, it is important to focus only on the basis of the question.

"Options" are the choices you have to answer the multiple-choice question. Often, the options require simple recognition of the right answer among a list of wrong answers. In more complex multiple-choice tests, all of the options can be similar or overlapping. You now have to narrow the options by reviewing the basis of the questions.

"Diversions" are sets of information designed to divert your attention or distract you from the basis of the question. The diversions can be either in the question or in the options. To stay focused, always return to the basis.

Absolutes and Trick Words

Be careful about statements that contain absolutes or words with fixed meanings. Always, never, none, and all are examples. Trick words are diversions most of the time. More, less, some, sometimes, not and except are examples of words that you need to stop and examine. Answers can appear to be obvious until you spot one of these words.

Reading and Comprehension Multiple-Choice Questions

Reading and reasoning type questions are looking to test your ability to understand the contents of a passage (usually three to four paragraphs long).

Before reading the passage, read the questions. Do NOT read the potential answers. If you are allowed, highlight or underline key words or phrases. This is especially important if you recognize information directly related to one of the questions about the passage.

Multiple-Choice Math Questions

Even though you are dealing in numbers, you want to approach math problems the same as word problems. What is the basis for the question? What is causing a diversion? What are the realistic (best guess, best estimate) options?

Read the options carefully. Often there will be several numbers that look alike that are obviously diversions. Work the problem before looking at the answers.

Graphs and Charts

Read the questions about the graph or chart first (not the answers). Review the chart. Start with the most obvious answer first. Translate the graph into words. Think through the graph in "real world" terms. Does the relationship between x and y make sense?

Short Answers

Short answer questions can show up in several forms:

- Fill in the blank
- A word in the middle of a sentence
- Complete the sentence
- Definitions

Short answer questions generally require specific, declarative or rote memory for completion. The best way to prepare for this type of test is with flash cards.

- Read the directions through completely. If you have questions about the directions, ask the teacher for clarification.
- Read the questions carefully. By only reading the first part of the question or scanning the question, you may jump to the wrong conclusion.
- Look for words that could give you a clue to the answer: a, an, the, these, those, they.
- Only answer what is asked. Writing out too much will waste valuable time and the information is probably not needed anyway. The exception is when you think of two or more possibilities. Go ahead and write them down. Flag the question. If you do not have time to get back to the question, a generous teacher may give you partial credit.

True/False Questions

In some cases, true/false questions are designed to test your knowledge of a specific subject. In most cases, however, you will be tested not only on the subject, but also on your ability to analyze or interpret factual information.

It is important to break the true/false questions into parts on both long and short statements. Do not, however, over analyze.

Absolutes and Trick Words

Watch for the absolutes and trick words as clues to answer. Negative words can be confusing. Cross out all pairs of negatives; i.e., this statement in not untrue. Reread the statement. It will make more sense.

As a general rule (not an absolute always), most answers on a true/false test are true. The only reason is that true statements are easier to write. If you have to guess, select true. Unless you are penalized for guessing, always guess. You have the same chances as flipping a coin.

ESSAY TESTS

Preparation - Prior to any essay test, it is important to guess the questions (see "real meaning" and "express your knowledge") Write out your answers the night before just as though you were taking the test. Time yourself based on the time you will have in class.

The Question - Read the question carefully. If allowed, underline key words in the question. If the question has multiple parts, use a learning map to recreate the question and its parts.

The Answer

The teacher will be looking for three key elements:

1. Your knowledge of the subject
2. Your ability to organize your thoughts
3. Your writing skills

The answer, therefore, should have three main parts:

1. Introduction
2. Body
3. Conclusion

Introduction - Using several words from the question, restate or interpret the question. Some questions leave room for interpretation. The body of the answer must reflect the logic behind your interpretation.

The introduction is also the outline for your answer By giving a short outline, it gives you a chance to mentally organize your thoughts for the body of the answer.

Body - Use transitional words or statements. These will come from the introduction. State your main ideas clearly and concisely. Avoid rambling. Support your ideas with concrete examples or definitions. If you find yourself getting off track, review the question or your introduction.

Conclusion - In summary, restate your main idea. Add how you proved your point. If the question requires, make a "what we can learn" type of statement. You may also conclude that there is a next step that should take place.

Check your work. Edit or add as needed.

TEST-TAKING SUMMARY

- FIRE-UP! Be prepared
- Relax
- Listen to the oral directions
- Read the directions carefully
- Read the questions carefully
- Write down key words, numbers or other reminders
- Manage your time
- Answer the question asked
- Check all answers
- Learn from mistakes and successes

WEB SUPPORT

FIRE-UP YOUR LEARNING

is a Web supported program

Go to: **www.fire-up.com**

for

news and updates

COMING SOON

- Your FIRE-UP Diary
- Bibliography
- Analytical Thinking
- Updates
- Multi-Mind Magazine
- Games
- Test Taking Strategies
- Creative Thinking
- FIRE-UP Forum

The above support for your FIRE-UP program is free for a period of one year from the date of activation.

ABOUT THE AUTHOR

Thomas Madden has been involved with the field of education for over twenty-five years. Tom has been Director of Training for a Fortune 100 food company and Executive Vice President of Human Resources Development for a major health and beauty care company. As Executive Vice President for a consulting firm specializing in instructional design and training, Tom has trained thousands of teachers and trainers throughout the world.

In 1998, Tom became President of the Accelerated Learning Institute located in Las Vegas, Nevada. He uses his Masters in Clinical Psychology to enhance an innovative approach to education that speeds learning and dramatically enhances retention. The Accelerated Learning methodology takes the best from whole-brain learning, total physical response strategies, and mind theory techniques.

Tom has written the **FIRE-UP Your Learning and FIRE-UP Your Teaching** in response to those who have attended the highly successful teacher training seminars. His books and seminars blend the latest theories with practical application. Tom's philosophy is not only to teach how a technique works, but also to teach why it works. By understanding why, the learner can personalize and readily apply the information.

"Using Accelerated Learning has put the pieces of the puzzle together for me. It has helped me to become a better teacher. I have a greater understanding of how my children learn best, and have in turn used the information to help them know how to efficiently learn and retain what they learn as they study independently of me. I have observed my daughters requiring less study time and having greater retention of materials studied. I know it comes from applying what we have learned in Accelerated Learning's material."

Becky Kunz
Homeschool Mom

"This extraordinary book gives students the easy-to-use techniques that will change their lives. The well documented, brain based methods will help all students gain the confidence in their abilities to learn any topic they choose and, as a result, raise their grades and self-esteem. Anyone looking for tools on "how to learn" will count this book among their most treasured..."

Pat Wyman, M.A.
Author, Learning vs. Training, Strategies that Bridge the Gap

"Tom Madden illustrates his ideas, based on both research and practical experience, with compelling examples that will accelerate the learning of every student. He is truly a master educator and if you read this book you will never again approach learning the same! Madden calls for a whole new way of learning and he provides a clear path of action for those who accept the challenge!"

Donna Clark, Coordinator
of Drug-Free Schools,
Houston , TX